SECOND EDITION

TOUCHSTONE

WORKBOOK 1

MICHAEL MCCARTHY

JEANNE MCCARTEN

HELEN SANDIFORD

CAMBRIDGE
UNIVERSITY PRESS

Shaftesbury Road, Cambridge CB2 8EA, United Kingdom

One Liberty Plaza, 20th Floor, New York, NY 10006, USA

477 Williamstown Road, Port Melbourne, VIC 3207, Australia

314–321, 3rd Floor, Plot 3, Splendor Forum, Jasola District Centre, New Delhi – 110025, India

103 Penang Road, #05-06/07, Visioncrest Commercial, Singapore 238467

Torre de los Parques, Colonia Tlacoquemécatl del Valle, Mexico City CP 03200, Mexico

Cambridge University Press & Assessment is a department of the University of Cambridge.

We share the University's mission to contribute to society through the pursuit of education, learning and research at the highest international levels of excellence.

www.cambridge.org
Information on this title: www.cambridge.org/9781107639331

First published 2005
Second Edition 2014

20

Printed in Great Britain by Ashford Colour Press Ltd.

A catalog record for this publication is available from the British Library.

ISBN 978-1-107-67987-0 Student's Book
ISBN 978-1-107-62792-5 Student's Book A
ISBN 978-1-107-65345-0 Student's Book B
ISBN 978-1-107-63933-1 Workbook
ISBN 978-1-107-67071-6 Workbook A
ISBN 978-1-107-69125-4 Workbook B
ISBN 978-1-107-68330-3 Full Contact
ISBN 978-1-107-66769-3 Full Contact A
ISBN 978-1-107-61366-9 Full Contact B
ISBN 978-1-107-64223-2 Teacher's Edition with Assessment Audio CD/CD-ROM
ISBN 978-1-107-61414-7 Class Audio CDs (4)

Additional resources for this publication at www.cambridge.org/touchstone2

Contents

1 All about you 2

2 In class 10

3 Favorite people............................... 18

4 Everyday life 26

5 Free time 34

6 Neighborhoods 42

7 Out and about 50

8 Shopping.. 58

9 A wide world 66

10 Busy lives 74

11 Looking back 82

12 Fabulous food 90

All about you

Lesson A Hello and good-bye

1 Meetings and greetings

Vocabulary | **A** Complete the conversations. Choose and write the best response.

1. A Hello.

   B _Hi._____

   (a.) Hi.

   b. Good-bye.

2. A Hi. I'm Ted.

   B _____

   a. Hi, I'm Lucille. Nice to meet you.

   b. See you next week.

3. A How are you?

   B _____

   a. I'm Kyle.

   b. I'm fine, thanks.

4. A Good-bye.

   B _____

   a. See you later.

   b. Thanks.

5. A Good night.

   B _____

   a. Hello.

   b. Bye. See you tomorrow.

6. A Hi. How are you?

   B _____

   a. Good, thanks. How are you?

   b. Have a nice day.

Vocabulary **B Complete the conversations with the expressions in the box.**

| Good night. | ✓Hello. | How are you? | Nice to meet you. |
| Have a good evening. | Hi. | I'm fine | See you |

1. Jack _____Hello.___ I'm Jack.
   Anna _____ I'm Anna.
   Jack _____

2. Sonia Hi, Julie. How are you?
   Julie Good. _____
   Sonia _____ , thanks.

3. Mike _____
   Koji Thanks. You too.

4. Joan _____
   Mary Bye. _____ tomorrow.

C Complete the instant message.

Instant Message

Sandra Good morning, Jenny.
Jenny __Good morning__ , Sandra.
Sandra _____ are you?
Jenny _____ , thanks. _____
Sandra Good.
Jenny See you later.
Sandra OK. _____ a nice day.
Jenny Thanks. _____ too.
Sandra Bye.

3

1 My name's Eva.

Vocabulary | Complete the conversation.

A   Good morning.

B   Good morning.

A   How are you?

B   I'm fine.

A   What's your __name__?

B   Eva Salazar.

A   How do you spell your _____ name?

B   It's S-A-L-A-Z-A-R.

A   And what's your _____ name?

B   Eva.

A   OK. How do you _____ Eva?

B   E-V-A.

A   And are you Ms., Miss, or _____ ?

B   Ms.

A   Thank you. Have a nice day.

B   Thanks. You too.

2 Your personal information

Vocabulary | Complete the form. Use your own information.

Touchstone English Club

NAME: _____

      First   Middle   Last

☐ single   ☐ married

CLASS: _____

ROOM: _____

TEACHER: _____

3 Are we in the same class?

Grammar **A Complete the conversation. Write *am* or *are*. Use contractions *'m* or *'re* where possible.**

Receptionist Hello. ___Are___ you here for
an English class?

Mi-Young Yes, I _____ . I'm Mi-Young.

Receptionist Mi-Young Lee? You _____ in Class C.

Mi-Young Thank you.

Sergio Hi. _____ I in Class C, too? I'm Sergio.

Receptionist Yes, you _____ .

Sergio So we _____ in the same class.

Receptionist Wait. _____ you Sergio Rodrigues?

Sergio No, I _____ not. I'm Sergio Lopes.

Receptionist Oh, you _____ in Class D.
You _____ not in the same class.

B Complete the conversation.

David Hi. _____ _____ Julia Kim?

Leti No, _____ _____ . I'm Leticia Martinez,
but everyone calls me Leti.

David Hi, Leti. I'm David. Nice to meet you.

Leti _____ _____ here for a dance class?

David Yes, _____ _____ . _____ _____
in the same class?

Leti Yes, _____ _____ . We're in Class A.

4 About you

Grammar **Answer the questions. Use your own information.**

1. Are you in an English class?

   _____

2. Are you in a French class?

   _____

3. How are you today?

   _____

4. Are you and your friends in the same English class?

   _____

5. Are you married?

   _____

1 What's the number?

Vocabulary **A** Write the numbers.

0	1	2	3	4	5
zero	_____	_____	_____	_____	_____

6	7	8	9	10
_____	_____	_____	_____	_____

B Complete the crossword puzzle.

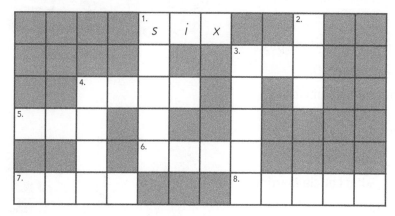

Across

1. two × three = ___six___

3. two + eight = _____

4. ten ÷ two = _____

5. six – four = _____

6. three + six = _____

7. five × zero = _____

8. six + two = _____

Down

1. ten – three = _____

2. eight – seven = _____

3. eight – five = _____

4. two × two = _____

2 What's the word?

Vocabulary The letters spell a word. Write each letter in the correct box below to see the word.

1. C	3. H	5. N	7. E	9. U
2. O	4. O	6. T	8. S	10. T

ten	four	nine	one	three	eight	six	two	five	seven
			C						

3 Here's your membership card.

Grammar | Look at Mark's student ID card. Write his answers in the conversation.

Lee   Hello. Are you a member of the club?

Mark No, I'm not.

Lee   OK. Well, here's an application form.
      So, what's your last name?

Mark *It's Brokaw.*   **or**   *Brokaw.*
      or *My last name's Brokaw.*

Lee   Thank you. And your first name?

Mark _____

Lee   What's your middle initial, please?

Mark _____

Lee   And what's your email address?

Mark _____

Lee   And your phone number?

Mark _____

Lee   Are you an English student?

Mark _____

Lee   What's your teacher's name?

Mark _____

Lee   Thank you. Here's your membership card.
      Have a nice day.

Student ID Card
Mark A. Brokaw

Telephone: 740-555-2968
Email: mab@cup.org
Department: English (Mrs. Roberts)

4 About you

Grammar and vocabulary | Write questions with *What's* and the words given. Then answer the questions with your own information.

1. A *What's your name?*
      (your name)

   B _____

2. A _____
      (your cell phone number)

   B _____

3. A _____
      (your email address)

   B _____

4. A _____
      (your English teacher's name)

   B _____

Are you here for the concert?

1 Good evening.

Complete the conversations with the expressions in the box. Use each expression only one time.

Good evening.	✓ Hi	How about you?	How are you doing?	Thank you.	Yes
Pretty good.	Hello.	Nice to meet you.	Good-bye.	thanks.	Yeah

1. Sam   Hi, Ali.

   Ali   ___*Hi*___ , Sam. _____

   Sam   Good, thanks. How about you?

   Ali   _____

   Sam   Am I late?

   Ali   _____ , you are, but it's OK.

   Sam   Good. By the way, here's your book.

   Ali   Oh, _____

2. Joe   Good evening.

   Clerk   _____ What's your name, please?

   Joe   Joe Johnson.

   Clerk   Oh, yes. Mr. Johnson. Your room number is
   10A. Here's your key.

   Joe   _____

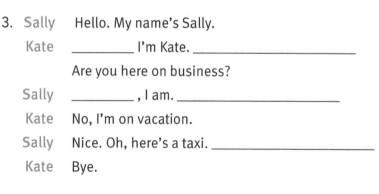

3. Sally   Hello. My name's Sally.

   Kate   _____ I'm Kate. _____

   Are you here on business?

   Sally   _____ , I am. _____

   Kate   No, I'm on vacation.

   Sally   Nice. Oh, here's a taxi. _____

   Kate   Bye.

2 How are you doing?

A **Rewrite the conversation. Use less formal expressions for the underlined words.**

A <u>Hello. How are you?</u>

B <u>I'm fine, thank you.</u> How are you?

A <u>I'm fine.</u> Are you a student here?

B <u>Yes,</u> I am. How about you?

A <u>Yes,</u> me too.

B What's the email address here?

A It's goodschool1@cup.org.

B <u>Thank you. Good-bye.</u>

A <u>Good-bye.</u>

A *Hi. How are you doing?*

B _____

A _____

B _____

A _____

B _____

A _____

B **Number the lines of the conversation in the correct order. Then write the conversation.**

____ Hi.

____ Yeah, me too.

____ OK.

____ Are you here for the concert?

____ How are you doing?

_1_ Hello.

____ Yeah, I am. How about you?

A *Hello.* _____

B _____

A _____

B _____

A _____

B _____

A _____

Unit 1 Progress chart

What can you do? Mark the boxes. ☑ = I can . . . ? = I need to review how to . . .	To review, go back to these pages in the Student's Book.
☐ make statements with *I'm (not)*, *you're (not)*, and *we're (not)*. ☐ ask questions with *Are you . . . ?* ☐ ask questions with *What's . . . ?* ☐ give answers with *It's . . . .*	2, 4, and 5 5 4, 6, and 7 6 and 7
☐ say *hello* and *good-bye* in at least 4 different ways. ☐ talk about names in English. ☐ use numbers 0–10.	1, 2, and 3 2 and 4 6
☐ use *How about you?* ☐ use everyday expressions in more formal and less formal situations.	8 9

Grammar (label for first group)
Vocabulary (label for second group)
Conversation strategies (label for third group)

1 Where is everybody today?

Grammar **A** Look at the pictures. Complete the sentences.

1. Bill _'s_____ at the gym.
   ___He's___ not at home.

2. Jon and Karen ___are___ at
   home. _____ not in class.

3. Sun-Yee _____ in the
   cafeteria. _____ late.

4. David _____ on vacation.
   _____ asleep.

5. Kate and Tess _____ in
   class. _____ not at the
   library.

6. Carmen _____ at work.
   _____ not sick.

B Complete the questions about the people in part A. Then answer the questions.

1. A _____Is____ Bill at work?
   B _No, he's not._____

2. A _____ Jon and Karen at home?
   B _____

3. A _____ Sun-Yee at the gym?
   B _____

4. A _____ David asleep?
   B _____

5. A _____ Kate and Tess on vacation?
   B _____

6. A _____ Carmen at work?
   B _____

② Absent classmates

Grammar | Complete the conversation with the verb *be*. Use contractions where possible.
Add *not* where necessary.

Silvia   Hi. How ____are____ you?

Jason   Good, thanks. How about you?

Silvia   Pretty good. _____ Dave here?

Jason   No, he _____ _____ .
I think he _____ sick.

Silvia   Oh. _____ he at home?

Jason   I don't know.

Silvia   How about Jenny and Paula?
_____ they here?

Jason   No, they _____ _____ . They _____
on vacation. I think they _____ in Miami.

Silvia   Look! Dave _____ not sick. He _____ over
there. He _____ just late again!

③ About you

Grammar and vocabulary | Complete the questions with the names of your friends and classmates.
Then answer the questions.

1. A Is ___Paul___ at home?
    B _Yes, he is._____

2. A Are _____ and _____ at work?
    B _____

3. A Is _____ in class today?
    B _____

4. A Are _____ and _____ on vacation?
    B _____

5. A Are _____ and _____ in your English class?
    B _____

6. A Is _____ sick today?
    B _____

7. A Is _____ at the library?
    B _____

8. A Are _____ and _____ asleep?
    B _____

11

1 Everyday things

Vocabulary | Label the things in the pictures. Use *a* or *an* where necessary.

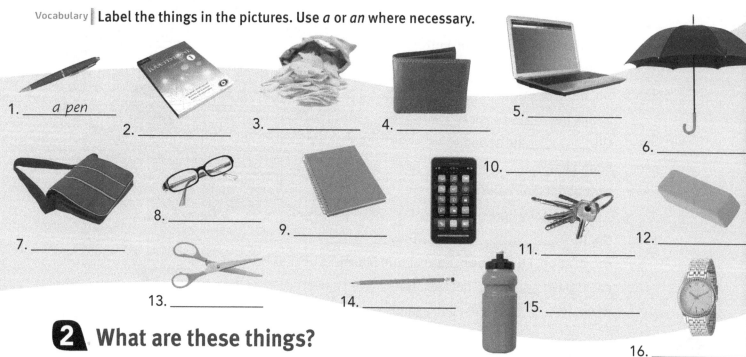

1. ___a pen___

2. _____

3. _____

4. _____

5. _____

6. _____

7. _____

8. _____

9. _____

10. _____

11. _____

12. _____

13. _____

14. _____

15. _____

16. _____

2 What are these things?

Grammar and vocabulary | Write sentences about the pictures.

1. ___This is a bag.___

2. ___These are pens.___

3. _____

4. _____

5. _____

6. _____

7. _____

8. _____

3 Asking about things

Grammar **Complete the conversations. Use the words in the box.**

Is	it	it's	these	they're	this	What
Is	it's	these	they	they're	this	✓What's

1.
    Clerk   You're in Room 102.

   Ms. Simms   Thanks. _*What's*_ this?

    Clerk   Oh, _____ your room key.

   Ms. Simms   OK. Thank you.

    Clerk   And _____ is your membership card for the fitness club.

2.
   Erica   What's _____ ? _____ it a smartphone?

   Jim   No, _____ not. It's a GPS.

   Erica   Oh.

   Jim   _____ are these?

   Erica   I think _____ watches.

3.
   Bob   What are _____ ?

   Jill   Oh, no! I think _____ my jeans.

   Bob   Oh, I'm sorry. Are _____ new?

   Jill   Yeah. Oh, look. _____ this your wallet?

   Bob   Yes, _____ is.

   Jill   Oh, no! And _____ are your credit cards!

1 Classroom things

Vocabulary **A** Write the words under the pictures. Use *a* or *some*.

1. ___a board___

2. ___some posters___

3. _____

4. _____

5. _____

6. _____

7. _____

8. _____

9. _____

10. _____

11. _____

12. _____

B Circle the words from part A in the puzzle. Look in these directions (→↓). Which word is *not* in the puzzle?

T	V	C	Q	U	A	B	L	A	M	A	B
W	E	H	A	S	I	P	U	Y	A	Z	O
A	C	A	L	E	N	D	A	R	P	H	A
G	O	I	H	K	O	B	Z	O	E	O	R
I	P	R	P	E	D	L	F	L	T	E	D
W	A	S	T	E	B	A	S	K	E	T	I
R	K	T	O	R	R	J	O	O	M	U	M
O	C	U	O	S	J	E	C	D	E	S	K
N	L	L	G	T	O	R	X	I	T	J	A
C	O	M	P	U	T	E	R	O	T	D	S
M	C	A	S	M	P	O	S	T	E	R	S
A	K	S	C	I	S	S	O	R	S	A	R

2 A classroom

Grammar
and
vocabulary

A Look at the picture. Complete the sentences. Use the words in the box.

in	in front of	in front of	next to	✓ on	on	on	under

1. The workbooks are ___on___ the table.
2. The calendar is _____ the wastebasket.
3. The computer is _____ the teacher's desk.
4. The map is _____ the window.

5. The students' papers are _____ the wall.
6. The teacher's desk is _____ the board.
7. The scissors are _____ the teacher's desk.
8. The table is _____ the chairs.

B Write the questions about the classroom in part A.

1. A _Where's the teacher's desk?_
   B It's in front of the board.

2. A _____
   B It's next to the window.

3. A _____
   B They're on the table.

4. A _____
   B They're under the teacher's desk.

5. A _____
   B They're on the wall.

6. A _____
   B It's in the wastebasket.

3 Missing apostrophes

Grammar Put apostrophes (') in the correct places in the questions. Then answer the questions.

1. What's on the wall in your classroom?   _____

2. What are your friends names?   _____

3. Whats your English teachers name?   _____

4. Wheres your teacher now?   _____

How do you spell it?

1 Questions, questions

Complete the conversations. Use the expressions in the box.

✓Excuse me   Thanks anyway.   Sure.   Here you go.   Thanks.
Can I borrow   You're welcome.   please   How do you spell   Sorry.
What's the word for this in English?

1. Callie   _Excuse me_ , Bob.

   Bob   Yeah?

   Callie   _____ your English book?

   Bob   Sure. Now, where is it?

   Callie   Um . . . it's right in front of you.

   Bob   Oh, yeah. _____

   Callie   Thanks.

   Bob   _____

2. Ruby   Can I borrow your cell phone,

   _____ ?

   Millie   _____ Oh, wait.

   It's not in my bag. I think it's at home.

   _____

   Ruby   That's OK. _____

   Millie   Sure. . . . _____

   Ruby   In English, the word is *umbrella*.

   Millie   Umbrella? Thanks.

   Ruby   Sure.

3. Yuri   _____ *computers*?

   Dan   C-O-M-P-U-T-E-R-S.

   Yuri   _____

   Dan   Sure.

   Yuri   And how do you spell *television*?

   Dan   T-V.

   Yuri   Very funny!

2 Scrambled conversations

Number the lines of the conversations in the correct order. Then write the conversations.

1. _____ I'm sorry.   A *You're late.* _____

   ___1___ You're late.   B _____

   _____ That's OK.   A _____

2. _____ Sure.   A _____

   _____ Thank you.   B _____

   _____ Can I borrow your pen, please?   A _____

   _____ You're welcome.   B _____

3. _____ I don't know.   A _____

   _____ That's OK. Thanks anyway.   B _____

   _____ That's OK. What about this? A _____

   _____ I'm sorry. I don't know.   B _____

   _____ What's the word for this?   A _____

Unit 2 Progress chart

What can you do? Mark the boxes. ✓ = I can . . . ? = I need to review how to . . .	To review, go back to these pages in the Student's Book.
Grammar	
☐ make statements with *he's (not)*, *she's (not)*, and *they're (not)*.	12 and 13
☐ ask questions with *Is he . . . ?*, *Is she . . . ?*, and *Are they . . . ?*	13
☐ use *a* or *an*.	14
☐ make nouns plural with *-s*, *-es*, or *-ies*.	15
☐ use *this* with singular nouns and *these* with plural nouns.	14 and 15
☐ ask questions with *Where . . . ?*	17
☐ use *'s* and *s'* to show possession.	17
Vocabulary	
☐ name at least 8 things students take to class.	14 and 15
☐ name at least 12 classroom items.	16 and 17
☐ say where things are in the classroom.	16 and 17
Conversation strategies	
☐ ask for help in class.	18
☐ use common responses to *Thank you* and *I'm sorry*.	19

Favorite people

1 Favorites

Vocabulary | **A** Unscramble the letters. Write the words.

1. rgiens   s _inger_

2. ctrao   a_____

3. rtweir   w_____

4. maet   t_____

5. ralype   p_____

6. dnab   b_____

7. prsot   s_____

8. naf   f_____

9. ivome   m_____

10. rtiats   a_____

B Complete the crossword puzzle with the words in part A.

Across

3. Adele is an amazing _____ .

5. Our favorite soccer _____ is Manchester United.

8. Hugh Jackman is a great _____ .

10. Ronaldo is a famous soccer _____ .

Down

1. Soccer is a _____ .

2. J.K. Rowling is a famous _____ .

4. Who's your favorite _____ ?

6. This _____ is exciting.

7. My favorite _____ is Coldplay.

9. Brian is a _____ of the Giants.

2 She's my favorite singer.

Grammar | Look at the pictures. Complete the sentences.

1. "_She's_ my favorite singer. _Her_ new album is great."

2. "_____ Jama fans. Jama is _____ favorite band."

3. "_____ a great writer. _____ new book is really good."

4. "_____ favorite movie is *The Aliens*. What's _____ favorite movie?"

5. "_____ my favorite actors. I think _____ movies are very good."

6. "Cassandra Coe is my teacher. _____ a great artist. _____ pictures are amazing."

3 They're great!

Grammar | Complete the conversation with the verb *be*. Use contractions where possible.

Alicia   I love this new Bruno Mars album. He _'s_ my favorite singer.

Norah   Yeah. I _____ a big fan of his, too. His voice _____ amazing. His songs _____ great.

Alicia   Yeah. So, what's your favorite band?

Norah   Maroon 5. They _____ great.

Alicia   Yes, they _____ very talented. Adam Levine _____ really good looking. He _____ my favorite.

1 What are they like?

Vocabulary | Look at the pictures. Complete the sentences. Use the words in the box.

busy	fun	lazy	✓quiet	smart	tired
friendly	interesting	outgoing	shy	strict	

1. She's _____quiet_____ and _____ .

2. He's _____ .

3. They're _____ .

4. She's _____ .

5. She's _____ .

6. He's _____ .

7. He's not very _____ or _____ .

8. They're _____ . She's _____ .

2 What's new?

Grammar | **Complete the conversation with the verb *be*. Use contractions where possible. Add *not* where necessary.**

Carrie   Sorry. ___*Am*___ I late?

Josh   No, you ____ _____ . You ____ fine.

Carrie   Good. So, what's new? _____ you busy at work?

Josh   Yes, I _____ . Our boss _____ sick, so he ____ _____ at work.

Carrie   Oh, really?

Josh   So, how about you? What _____ your new neighbors like? _____ they nice?

Carrie   Yes, they _____ . They _____ OK. They _____ very quiet.

Josh   _____ they students?

Carrie   No, they ____ _____ . The guy _____ a writer.

Josh   A writer? What about the woman? _____ she a writer, too?

Carrie   No, she ____ _____ . She ____ _____ a writer – she _____ a teacher. At our school!

3 Make it negative.

Grammar | **Rewrite the sentences in the negative form. Use contractions where possible.**

1. My neighbors are very nice.   *My neighbors aren't very nice.* _____

2. My best friend is a student.   _____

3. I'm very shy.   _____

4. The students in my class are very smart.   _____

5. My English class is easy.   _____

6. My teacher is very quiet.   _____

4 About you

Grammar and vocabulary | **Complete the questions. Then write short answers. Add more information.**

1. ___*Are*___ you outgoing?   *Yes, I am. I'm very outgoing.* _____

    or   *No, I'm not. I'm not outgoing.* _____

2. _____ your best friend lazy?   _____

3. _____ your English class hard?   _____

4. _____ your friends smart?   _____

5. _____ your teacher fun?   _____

6. _____ your classmates nice?   _____

7. _____ you tired today?   _____

8. _____ you and your friends busy after class?   _____

1 Who's who?

Vocabulary | Use the family tree to complete the sentences about this family.

1. David is Paul's ___son___ .
2. John is Katy's _____ .
3. Katy is Paul's _____ .
4. Josh, David, and Emily are Paul and Katy's _____ .
5. Emily is Josh's _____ .
6. Josh is David's _____ .
7. John and Catherine are Katy's _____ .
8. Katy is Josh's _____ .
9. John is Catherine's _____ .
10. Emily is Katy's _____ .
11. Catherine is David's _____ .
12. John is Emily's _____ .
13. Susan is David's _____ .
14. Bill is Josh's _____ .
15. Robert is Emily's _____ .

2 What's the number?

Vocabulary | Write the numbers.

65
1. ___sixty-five___

11
2. _____

24
3. _____

15
4. _____

16
5. _____

91
6. _____

56
7. _____

77
8. _____

3 How about your children?

Grammar and vocabulary **Complete the conversations. Write the full questions.**

1. A How / your parents?

   How are your parents?

   B They're fine. Thanks. How / your mom?

   _____

   A She's good. She's on vacation right now.

2. A What / your sisters' names?

   _____

   B Beth and Kate. My brother's name is Pete.

   A Pete? Oh, how old / he?

   _____

   B He's 21.

3. A Who / this?

   _____

   B Oh, it's my aunt.

4. A My cousins are really fun.

   B Yeah? How old / they?

   _____

   A They're my age.

5. A Where / your family today?

   _____

   B At home. How about your family?

   A They're at home, too.

6. A Where / you from?

   _____

   B Well, my parents are from Italy originally.

   A Really? Where / your parents from in Italy?

   _____

   B They're from Rome.

4 A famous family

Grammar **Read part of a phone interview with an actor. Then write questions for the answers.**

Interviewer	Hello, Kate. How are you?
Kate	Hi. I'm fine, thanks.
Interviewer	Kate, I love your movies.
Kate	Thank you.
Interviewer	Now, about your family . . . who's your mother?
Kate	Gwen Russell – the artist. And Kevin Russell is my father.
Interviewer	Yes, they're famous! What are your parents like at home?
Kate	Oh, Dad's fun and outgoing. And Mom's very smart!
Interviewer	And, Kate, what's your favorite band?
Kate	Imagine Dragons. They're amazing. . . .

1. *How is Kate?*

   She's fine.

2. _____

   Her mother is Gwen Russell.

3. _____

   Her father is fun and outgoing. Her mother is very smart.

4. _____

   Her favorite band is Imagine Dragons.

Lesson D / A songwriter? Really?

1 New neighbors and co-workers

Conversation strategies | Complete the conversations with the questions in the box.

| How old is she? | Where is she from? | ✓What are they like? | An actor? Is she good? |
| From Chile? | Are they friendly? | Are they good? | Where are they from? |

1. **Ming** Who are they?

   Jim Oh, they're my new neighbors.

   Ming Your neighbors? _What are they like?_

   Jim Interesting. Very interesting. They're in a rock band.

   Ming A rock band? _____

   Jim They're from New York.

   Ming Wow! _____

   Jim No, they're not.

   Ming Uh-oh. _____

   Jim Oh, very. Their friends are always here!

2. **Carlos** Who's she?

   Kim Her name's Angie.

   Carlos Angie? _____

   Kim I don't know exactly. I think she's from Chile.

   Carlos _____ Really?

   What's she like?

   Kim She's outgoing and fun.

   Carlos Really? _____

   Kim I'm not sure. Maybe 24 or 25.

   Carlos Oh. What's her job? Is she a server here?

   Kim Well, yes. But she's an actor, too.

   Carlos _____

   Kim Yeah, she's a good actor but not a great server.

2 Really? I'm surprised!

Write responses to show you are interested or surprised. Then ask a question.

1. My grandmother's name is Banu.

   Really? What's she like? _____

2. My brother is a singer in a band.

   _____

3. My grandfather is a tennis player.

   _____

4. I'm from Alaska.

   _____

5. My mother is a Spanish teacher.

   _____

6. My new job is hard work.

   _____

7. My sister is an artist.

   _____

8. My last name is Oh.

   _____

Unit 3 Progress chart

What can you do? Mark the boxes. ☑ = I can . . . ? = I need to review how to . . .	To review, go back to these pages in the Student's Book.
☐ use *my*, *your*, *his*, *her*, *our*, and *their*.	22 and 23
☐ make statements with *be*.	22 and 23
☐ ask *yes-no* questions with *be*.	24 and 25
☐ make negative statements with *be*.	24 and 25
☐ ask information questions with *be*.	26 and 27
☐ name at least 8 words to describe people's personalities.	24 and 25
☐ name at least 12 family words.	26 and 27
☐ say numbers 10–101.	26
☐ show interest by repeating information and asking questions.	28
☐ use *Really?* to show interest or surprise.	29

Grammar

Vocabulary

Conversation strategies

Everyday life

Lesson A / In the morning

 1 **What's Kathy's morning like?**

Grammar and vocabulary

A Complete the sentences about Kathy's morning. Use the correct form of the verbs in the box.

check	exercise	✓get up	play
eat	get up	listen	read

1. Kathy _gets up_ early. Her son _____ late.

2. She _____ before work. Her son _____ games.

3. She _____ to the radio in the car.

4. She and her co-workers _____ breakfast together.

5. Kathy _____ her email right after breakfast.

6. Her boss _____ the newspaper at work.

B Rewrite the sentences in the negative form. Use contractions where possible.

1. Kathy's son gets up early. _Kathy's son doesn't get up early._

2. Kathy checks her email before breakfast. _____

3. Kathy and her son talk a lot in the morning. _____

4. Kathy's son does his homework. _____

5. Kathy and her boss eat breakfast together. _____

6. Kathy's boss plays computer games. _____

2 Guess what!

Grammar **Complete Peter's email with the correct form of the verbs.**

> **New Message**
>
> To: Samir22@cup.com
> From: PeterJ@cup.com
> Subject: **New Job**
>
> Hi!
>
> Guess what! I ___have___ (have) a new job – in a coffee shop. It's hard work. I _____ (get up) early, and I _____ (work) late. But the coffee is good.
>
> My boss is nice. He's French, and he _____ (study) English at night. He _____ (do) his homework in the coffee shop. I _____ (help) him sometimes. He's quiet, and he _____ (not / talk) a lot. He _____ (listen) to the radio and _____ (sing), but we _____ (not / like) the same music. He _____ (like) coffee, too. We both _____ (have) four cups of coffee every day!
>
> Write soon!
>
> Peter

3 Typical morning activities

Grammar and vocabulary **A What are typical morning activities? Match the verbs with the words and expressions.**

1. do _d_
2. study ____
3. check ____
4. listen ____
5. drive ____
6. play ____
7. read ____
8. go ____

a. to the radio
b. (my) email or messages
c. a car
✓d. (my) homework
e. on the Internet
f. English
g. games on the computer
h. a book

B Write true sentences about your morning routine. Use the verbs in part A.

1. _I don't do my homework in the morning._
2. _____
3. _____
4. _____
5. _____
6. _____
7. _____
8. _____

1 What's fun? What's not?

Vocabulary **A** Which routine activities are fun for you? Complete the charts. Add your own ideas.

check email	do the laundry	go shopping	take a class
clean the house	eat snacks	make phone calls	text friends
do homework	get up early	✓ play sports	watch TV

Fun!	
play sports	

Not fun!	

B Write the days of the week in the date book. Then write one thing you do each day.

S *unday* : *I go shopping on Sundays.* **Th**_____ : _____

M_____ : _____ **F**_____ : _____

T_____ : _____ **S**_____ : _____

W_____ : _____

2 About you 1

Grammar and vocabulary **Use time expressions to write one thing you do and one thing you don't do.**

1. on the weekends   *I clean the house on the weekends.*
   I don't go to work on the weekends.

2. after work / class   _____
   _____

3. every day   _____
   _____

4. on Saturdays   _____
   _____

5. in the afternoons   _____
   _____

6. at night   _____
   _____

3 What's your week like?

Grammar | **Complete the conversation with the correct form of the verbs.**

Cecilia   What's your week like, Eduardo? __Do__ (Do / Does)

you __go__ to work every day?
(go / goes)

Eduardo   Well, no, I _____ . I work at home on Fridays.
(don't / doesn't)

Cecilia   Really? What about on the weekends? _____
(Do / Does)

you _____ then, too?
(work / works)

Eduardo   Yes, I _____ . But I don't like it. What
(do / does)

about you? _____ you and your husband
(Do / Does)

_____ to work every day?
(go / goes)

Cecilia   Yes, we _____ . But just Monday to Friday.
(do / does)

We _____ the house on the weekends.
(clean / cleans)

Oh, and we _____ to soccer games.
(go / goes)

Eduardo   Oh. _____ your son _____ soccer?
(Do / Does)   (play / plays)

Cecilia   Yes, he _____ . He's on the school team.
(do / does)

_____ your son _____ any sports?
(Do / Does)   (play / plays)

Eduardo   No, he _____ . He plays games on his computer.
(don't / doesn't)

4 About you 2

Grammar and vocabulary | **Complete the questions. Then write answers with your own information.**

1. A ___Do___ you ___take___ a class at night?
    B _Yes, I do. I take a Spanish class on Monday evenings._

2. A _____ your father _____ the laundry on weekends?
    B _____

3. A _____ you and your friends _____ shopping on Saturdays?
    B _____

4. A _____ your friends _____ their email before breakfast?
    B _____

5. A _____ your mother _____ the news on the Internet every day?
    B _____

1 Saying more than *yes* or *no*

Conversation strategies **A** Complete the conversation. Use the sentences in the box.

> I work part-time in the cafeteria.   It's fun, and the people are nice.
> Just Mondays and Wednesdays.   I'm an English student.
> ✓ I'm new here, and I'm late.   I go there Mondays after work. It's great!

Mike   Hi. Are you OK? You look lost.

Yumi   Hello. Where's Room 106? Do you know?
   I'm new here, and I'm late.

Mike   Yeah. It's right over there, next to the cafeteria.

Yumi   Thanks. So, do you work here?

Mike   Yes, I do. _____

Yumi   Do you like the job?

Mike   Yeah, I do. _____

Yumi   That's good. Do you work here every day?

Mike   Well, no. _____
   I go to class on Tuesdays and Thursdays.

Yumi   Oh. So you're a student, too?

Mike   Yeah. _____

Yumi   Really? I'm an English student, too. Do you belong
   to the English Club?

Mike   Yes, I do. _____

Yumi   Oh. Well, thanks a lot. And see you at English Club!

Mike   Great!

B Read the completed conversation again. Then read the sentences below.
Check (✓) *T* (true) or *F* (false).

	T	F
1. Mike and Yumi are friends.	☐	☑
2. Mike works in the cafeteria.	☐	☐
3. Mike is a new student.	☐	☐
4. Mike works Tuesdays and Thursdays.	☐	☐
5. Mike likes his part-time job.	☐	☐
6. Yumi and Mike are English students.	☐	☐
7. Mike belongs to the English Club.	☐	☐

2 About you

Conversation strategies **Unscramble the questions. Then answer the questions. Write more than *yes* or *no*. Use *Well* if you need to.**

1. live / you / around / Do / here ?

   Do you live around here?

2. from / originally / you / here / Are ?

3. a / full-time / you / Are / student ?

4. have / you / brothers / Do / sisters / or ?

5. you / work / the / on / weekends / Do ?

6. Do / your / every day / text / friends / you ?

7. get up / day / you / Do / every / early ?

8. grandparents / Do / with / your / live / you ?

1 Watching TV

Reading **A** What do you think average Americans do after work and school?
Check (✓) three boxes.

☐ spend time with family ☐ read ☐ watch TV
☐ go out with friends ☐ go out to dinner ☐ go shopping

B Read the article. Check your answers in part A.

After WORK and SCHOOL

Do Americans go out every night after work and have fun? Maybe the answer is surprising, but no, they don't. They don't usually go out with friends in the evening, and they don't go out to dinner or go shopping. So what do they do? Well, about 90% of Americans stay at home in the evening to relax. In fact, it's their favorite activity. They read, watch TV, and spend time with their families.

So what about young people? Well, they spend a lot of time at home, too. American high school students study about six hours a week and watch TV for about 15 hours a week.

Most Americans also have a hobby and do fun, interesting things like play sports or music. Americans stay home a lot, but they stay busy, too!

Here are average Americans' favorite activities:

* reading
* watching TV
* spending time with their families
* exercising
* using the Internet

TV Set

C Read the article again. Then correct these false sentences.

1. Americans go out with friends every night after work.
   Americans don't usually go out with friends in the evening.

2. After work, Americans usually go shopping.
   _____

3. American high school students usually study for three hours a night.
   _____

4. American high school students don't watch TV.
   _____

5. The average American doesn't have a hobby.
   _____

2 Weekends

Writing **A Read the email messages. Then rewrite Joe's message. Use capital letters and periods.**

New Message

Hi Joe,
Are you busy on weekends?
I am. On Friday nights, I go to
a club in Miami. On
Saturdays, I sleep late. In the
evening, I watch TV. On
Sundays, I study. Do you
study on the weekends?
Ian

New Message

hi ian,
yes, i have busy weekends on
friday nights, i visit my family
downtown on saturdays,
i take a spanish class at grove
college on sundays, i play
soccer i don't study on
weekends – i don't have time
joe

New Message

Hi Ian,
_____
_____
_____
_____
_____
_____
_____
_____

B What do you do on weekends? Write an email to a friend about your weekend activities.

New Message

Hi _____ ,
_____
_____
_____
_____
_____
_____
_____

Unit 4 Progress chart

What can you do? Mark the boxes. ✔ = I can . . . ? = I need to review how to . . .	To review, go back to these pages in the Student's Book.
Grammar	
☐ make simple present statements.	34 and 35
☐ ask simple present *yes-no* questions and give short answers.	36 and 37
Vocabulary	
☐ name at least 12 new verbs for routine activities.	34, 35, 36, and 37
☐ name the days of the week.	36
☐ name at least 8 time expressions with the simple present.	37
Conversation strategies	
☐ answer questions with more than *yes* or *no*.	38 and 39
☐ use *Well* to get time to think of an answer.	39
Writing	
☐ use capital letters and periods.	41

Free time

Lesson A / Going out

1 In your free time

Vocabulary | How often do you do these things? Complete the chart with the free-time activities in the box. Add your own ideas.

✓ eat out	go out with friends	go to a club	go to the gym	play a sport
go on the Internet	go shopping	go to a movie	have dinner with family	text family

every day	three or four times a week	once or twice a week	once or twice a month
		eat out	

2 Craig's busy schedule

Grammar and vocabulary | A Read Craig's weekly planner. Are the sentences below true or false? Write *T* (true) or *F* (false). Then correct the false sentences.

WEEKLY PLANNER

SUNDAY	MONDAY	TUESDAY	WEDNESDAY	THURSDAY	FRIDAY	SATURDAY
5	**6**	**7**	**8**	**9**	**10**	**11**
morning: do the laundry!!	morning: classes	morning: go to the gym!	morning: classes	morning: go to the gym!	morning: classes	morning: clean the house!!
	afternoon: go shopping	afternoon: library	afternoon: guitar lesson			afternoon: tennis with Bob
evening: dinner with Mom and Dad				evening: dinner with Sandra	evening: movie with Jim	evening: club with Bill

             three evenings a week

1. He goes out with friends ~~every evening~~. __F__

2. He goes to the library every day. _____

3. He goes shopping once a week. _____

4. He takes guitar lessons on Wednesday mornings. _____

5. He plays tennis twice a week. _____

6. He does the laundry three times a week. _____

7. He sees his parents on the weekends. _____

8. He cleans the house on Saturday mornings. _____

Grammar **B** **Now answer these questions about Craig's schedule.**

1. How often does he go to the gym?   *He goes to the gym twice a week.*
2. When does he have classes?   _____
3. How often does he go to a club?   _____
4. What does he do on Thursday evenings?   _____
5. When does he go to the movies?   _____
6. What does he do on Saturday afternoons?   _____
7. Who does he play tennis with?   _____
8. Where does he go on Saturday evenings?   _____

3 About you

Grammar
and
vocabulary | **Write questions for a friend. Then answer your friend's questions.**

1. You   *Where do you go after class?*
        (go after class)

   Friend   I meet some friends and go to a restaurant for dinner.
   How about you?

   You   _____

2. You   _____
        (text your friends)

   Friend   Every day. But I don't text before breakfast. How about you?

   You   _____

3. You   _____
        (do in your free time at home)

   Friend   I rent a movie, or I just relax in front of the TV with a friend.
   How about you?

   You   _____

4. You   _____
        (go on the weekends)

   Friend   I go to a restaurant or club. How about you?

   You   _____

5. You   _____
        (go out with)

   Friend   Oh, friends from school. How about you?

   You   _____

1 How often?

Grammar | **A** Write the frequency adverbs in order in the chart below.

✓always   hardly ever   never   often   sometimes   usually

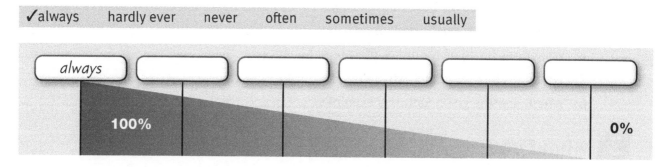

always

100%   0%

B Answer the questions. Write true sentences using frequency adverbs.

What's something you . . .

1. hardly ever do before school or work?   _I hardly ever check my email before school._
2. always do in the morning?   _____
3. sometimes do after school or work?   _____
4. never do during dinner?   _____
5. often do in the evening?   _____
6. usually do on Saturdays?   _____

2 What kinds of TV shows do you know?

Vocabulary | **A** Look at the pictures. Circle the correct type of TV show.

1. (soap opera)/
   the news

2. talk show /
   cartoon

3. sitcom /
   the news

4. cartoon /
   game show

5. documentary /
   talk show

6. talk show /
   cartoon

7. sitcom /
   reality show

8. the news /
   game show

B Circle the kinds of TV shows from part A in the puzzle. Look in these directions (→↓).

T	C	S	I	T	C	O	M	E	T	I	S
E	A	O	E	D	H	P	O	R	H	I	H
L	R	E	A	L	I	T	Y	S	H	O	W
K	T	A	L	K	S	H	O	W	U	P	O
S	O	A	P	O	P	E	R	A	E	E	U
D	O	C	U	M	E	N	T	A	R	Y	N
A	N	O	O	T	H	E	J	E	I	W	S
Y	T	E	A	I	U	W	D	O	C	T	V
Y	C	G	A	M	E	S	H	O	W	L	Y

3 About you

Grammar
and
vocabulary | **Answer the questions. Give two pieces of your own information in each answer.**

1. Do you ever watch soap operas? *Yes, I usually watch soap operas in the afternoons.*
   I love the stories.

2. What sitcoms do you hardly ever watch? _____

3. How often do you watch documentaries? _____

4. What talk shows do you like? _____

5. When do you usually watch the news? _____

6. How often do you watch reality shows? _____

1 Asking questions in two ways

Conversation strategies Complete the conversations with the questions in the box.

Do you like French?   I mean, do you belong to any clubs?
✓ Do you do anything special?   I mean, do you know a nice place?
Do you play baseball?   I mean, do you go every day?

1. Lisa   What do you do after work?
   Do you do anything special?

   Debbie   Well, I go to the gym.

   Lisa   Really? How often do you go?
   _____

   Debbie   No, not every day. I go Mondays, Wednesdays, and Thursdays.

2. Howard   Do you know the restaurants around here?
   _____

   Mary   Well, I often go to a little place on Main Street. What kind of food do you like?
   _____

   Howard   Yes, I do. I love French food.

3. Paul   What do you do after school?
   _____

   Tom   Well, yeah. I'm in the Sports Club.
   Paul   Really? What do you play?
   _____

   Tom   Well, no. We watch baseball on TV!
   Paul   Oh.

2 Questions, questions

Conversation strategies | **Write a second question for each question below. Then write true answers.**

1. What's your teacher like?
I mean, is she nice?

Yes, she's very nice. She's friendly.

2. How often do you have English class?

3. How do you get to school / work?

4. What do you do for fun on the weekends?

5. Do you read a lot?

6. Do you ever go to clubs?

3 About you

Conversation strategies | **Add frequency adverbs to make these sentences true for you.
Then use *I mean*, and write more information.**

1. I <u>never</u> go to the gym. *I mean, I usually exercise at home.*

2. I _____ get home early. _____

3. I _____ see my friends during the week. _____

4. I _____ go on the Internet in the evening. _____

5. I _____ eat breakfast at school / work. _____

6. I _____ get up early. _____

7. I _____ eat out on Saturdays. _____

8. I _____ watch reality shows on TV. _____

9. I _____ go shopping on the weekends. _____

10. I _____ study English after dinner. _____

1 Paula's problem

Reading **A** Read Paula's post to an online forum. How many hours does Paula spend online?

☐ 3 or 4 hours ☐ 4 or 5 hours ☐ 8 or 9 hours

○ ○ ○

PaulaT18 posted 2 hours ago

I live with my parents and my two brothers. They say I hardly ever spend time with them. My parents say I spend too much time on my phone and in front of my computer, but I don't think that's true. I mean, I often get up early and check my messages, but we always eat breakfast together. I guess I sometimes text during breakfast, but I never call people then. After class, I listen to music on my phone, but I also do my homework. In the evening, I often log on to my social network to chat with friends. They're always online. Sometimes I watch a movie on my computer. I usually spend eight or nine hours online every day. I don't think it's a problem. What do you think?

B Read Paula's post again. Then answer the questions.

1. Who does Paula live with? *She lives with her parents and her two brothers.*

2. Is she a student? _____

   _____

3. When does she log on to her social network? _____

   _____

4. What does Paula use her phone and computer for? _____

   _____

   _____

5. What do you think? Does Paula have a problem? Why or why not?

   _____

   _____

   _____

2 I need some advice!

Writing **A Read José's post to an online forum. Complete it with *and* or *but*.**

○ ○ ○

José   posted 2 hours ago

I think I have a problem. I don't have a computer at home, ___*but*___ I use a computer at school. I usually go to school early, _____ I check my email. I send email to my friends in other countries. I often go online for fun, _____ sometimes I study English on the computer. Then on the weekends, I go to school _____ write papers for class (on the computer). Do I spend too much time at school?

B   Write a post for an online forum about a problem you have. Write about a problem below, or use your own idea.

"I watch too much TV."   "I go shopping too much."   "I work too much."

"I stay home too much."   "I talk on my cell phone too much."   "I study too much."

○ ○ ○

_____

_____

_____

_____

_____

_____

Unit 5 Progress chart

What can you do? Mark the boxes. ✓ = I can . . . ? = I need to review how to . . .	To review, go back to these pages in the Student's Book.
Grammar □ ask simple present information questions.	44 and 45
□ use time expressions like *once a week*.	44 and 45
□ use frequency adverbs like *sometimes*, *never*, etc.	46
Vocabulary □ name at least 6 new free-time activities.	44 and 45
□ name at least 6 kinds of TV shows.	47
□ talk about likes and dislikes.	47
Conversation strategies □ ask questions in 2 ways to be less direct.	48
□ use *I mean* to repeat an idea and say more.	49
Writing □ use *and* and *but* to link ideas.	51

Neighborhoods

Lesson A / Nice places

1 What's in the neighborhood?

Vocabulary | Label the places in the picture. Use the words in the box with *a / an* or *some*.

✓apartment buildings	fast-food places	museum	park	restaurants	supermarket
club	movie theater	outdoor café	post office	stores	swimming pool

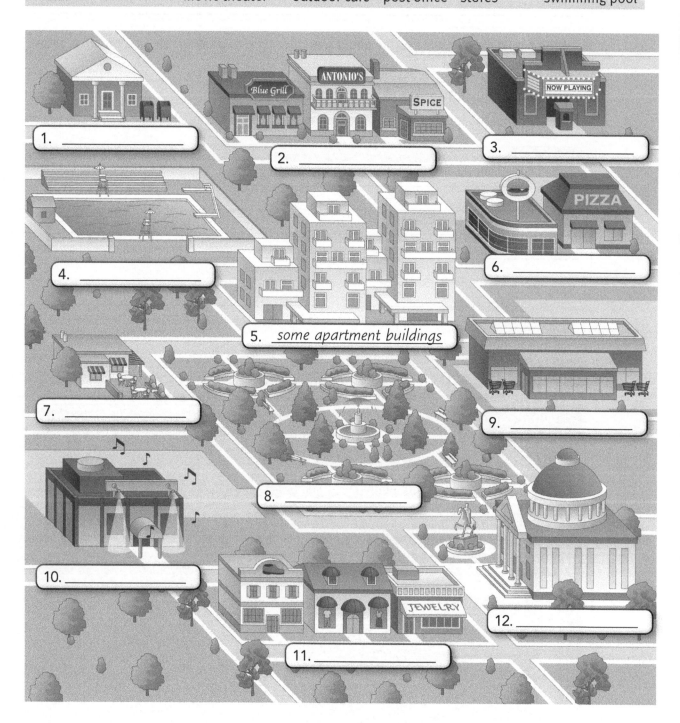

1. _____

2. _____

3. _____

4. _____

5. *some apartment buildings*

6. _____

7. _____

8. _____

9. _____

10. _____

11. _____

12. _____

2 Can you find the opposites?

Vocabulary | **Find six pairs of adjective opposites in the box. Write them in the chart below.**

bad	boring	expensive	interesting	noisy	quiet
big	cheap	good	✓ new	✓ old	small

new – old

3 That's not quite right!

Grammar | **Look at the picture on page 42. Correct the sentences to describe the neighborhood.**

1. There's one cheap fast-food place.   *There are a couple of cheap fast-food places.*

2. There are a couple of post offices. _____

3. There's a big stadium. _____

4. There are a couple of supermarkets. _____

5. There are some malls. _____

6. There's an apartment building. _____

7. There are no small stores. _____

8. There's an expensive restaurant. _____

9. There are a lot of beautiful parks. _____

10. There's no movie theater. _____

4 About you

Grammar and vocabulary | **What's your neighborhood like? Complete the sentences with true information.**

1. There's a _____ .

2. There are a lot of _____ .

3. There are some _____ .

4. There are a couple of _____ .

5. There's no _____ .

6. There are no _____ .

1 What's the time?

Vocabulary **A Write the times in words. Where there are two lines, write the times two ways.**

1. *It's twelve p.m.*
   It's noon.

2. _____
   _____

3. _____

4. _____

5. _____
   _____

6. _____
   _____

B Read about Kayo's day. Write the times in numbers. Then number the sentences in the correct order.

_____ Her bus comes at __*7:55*__ (five to eight).

_____ She gets home at _____ (nine fifteen) and watches TV.

__*1*__ Kayo gets up at _____ (six twenty-five).

_____ She goes for lunch with her co-workers at _____ (noon).

_____ She starts work at _____ (eight forty-five).

_____ She meets her boyfriend at _____ (twenty five to six), and they have dinner.

_____ She eats breakfast at _____ (twenty after seven).

_____ She leaves work at _____ (ten after five).

_____ She goes to bed at _____ (ten thirty).

2 Let's do it!

Grammar **Complete the conversations. Write questions starting with *What time . . . ?*
Use *Let's* to end each conversation with a suggestion.**

1. A I'm starving. Let's go to Burger Queen.

   B But it's late. <u>*What time does it close?*</u>

   A It closes around 11:00, I think. _____

   B Almost 10:00. _____

2. A There's a new reality show on TV tonight.

   B _____

   A Um, I think it starts at 8:00.

   B Well, I'm really tired. _____

   A I'm not sure. I think it ends at 9:30.

   B OK. _____

3. A Let's go to the gym on Saturday morning.

   B Sure. _____

   A Oh, it opens early. At 6:00. _____

   B I usually get up around 8:00 on Saturdays.

   A OK. _____

3 About you

Grammar
and
vocabulary **Unscramble the questions. Then write true answers.**

1. do / What time / get up / on weekdays / you ?

   A <u>*What time do you get up on weekdays?*</u>

   B _____

2. your family / have / What time / does / lunch / on Sundays ?

   A _____

   B _____

3. your English class / What time / start / does ?

   A _____

   B _____

4. What time / leave home / do / you / in the morning ?

   A _____

   B _____

5. stores / do / What time / in your neighborhood / open and close ?

   A _____

   B _____

1 Responses

Conversation strategies | Circle the two correct responses to each comment. Cross out the incorrect response.

1. I think every neighborhood needs a park.
   a. ~~Me neither.~~
   b. (Me too.)
   c. (Right.)

2. We don't have a good fast-food place here.
   a. Yeah.
   b. Me too.
   c. I know.

3. I don't like the new restaurant.
   a. Yeah. I know.
   b. Me neither.
   c. Me too.

4. There are no good bookstores around here.
   a. I know.
   b. Me too.
   c. Right.

5. I like the new outdoor café downtown.
   a. Me neither.
   b. Me too.
   c. Right. It's good.

6. I love this neighborhood. It's so quiet.
   a. Right.
   b. Yeah, I know.
   c. Me neither.

2 What do they have in common?

Conversation strategies | Read the conversation. Are the sentences below true or false? Write *T* (true) or *F* (false).

Glen   What's your new neighborhood like?

Anna   Oh, it's amazing. There are a lot of outdoor cafés and movie theaters and clubs. I go out a lot.

Glen   Really? I hardly ever go out in my neighborhood. It's boring.

Anna   Let's do something in my neighborhood this weekend. I'm free on Saturday.

Glen   Me too.

Anna   Well, there's a great jazz club near my apartment. I love jazz.

Glen   Really? Me too!

Anna   But let's have dinner at a café first. The food at the club is expensive, and I don't have a lot of money.

Glen   Me neither. So, let's meet at 6:30 at your apartment.

1. Glen and Anna both like their neighborhoods. __F__

2. Glen and Anna both go out a lot in their neighborhoods. ____

3. Glen and Anna are both free on Saturday. ____

4. Glen and Anna both love jazz. ____

5. Glen and Anna both have a lot of money. ____

> ✏ **Help note**
>
> Glen and Anna **both** love jazz.
> Glen loves jazz, **and** Anna loves jazz, **too**.

3 Right. I know.

Conversation strategies Circle the expression that is true about your neighborhood. Then show you agree. Respond with *Right* or *I know*.

1. A (There are some) / There are no good restaurants in my neighborhood.

   B *I know.* _____

2. A My neighborhood **has / doesn't have** a lot of great stores.

   B _____

3. A I live in a **great / terrible** neighborhood.

   B _____

4. A We **need / don't need** a shopping mall around here.

   B _____

4 About you

Conversation strategies Imagine you're talking to people from your neighborhood. Write true responses.

1. I really like this neighborhood.

   Me too. I think it's great.
   or
   Really? I don't like it very much.

2. I don't eat out in this neighborhood.

   _____

3. I think the restaurants are very expensive here.

   _____

4. I don't know a lot of people around here.

   _____

5. I think our neighborhood is boring.

   _____

6. I think we need a couple of new stores in our neighborhood.

   _____

1 Free weekend events!

Reading | **A** Read about some local events on a website. Match the pictures with the events. Write the correct numbers next to the pictures.

Downtown Weekend Section

* * * FREE EVENTS * * *

1. All Day Music Meet local bands, singers, and musicians at City Park this Sunday. Listen to great music, dance to pop songs, or take a music workshop and write your own song! The music starts at 3 p.m. and finishes at 11 p.m. Call Melissa at 555-9075 for more information.

2. Spring Food Festival Do you love food? Do you often eat out? Then come to the Parkview Food Festival. Eat some delicious food from 20 different restaurants around the neighborhood – all for FREE!
Saturday from 11:00 a.m. to 4:00 p.m. at Green Street Park.

3. Outdoor Street Fair *Saturday and Sunday from 10:00 a.m. to 6:00 p.m. in front of the City Art Museum.* There are a lot of beautiful items for sale – books, art, photos, paintings, clothes, and more. Items for sale are just $2–$25. Coffee, sodas, and snacks are for sale, too!

4. Free Classes at the Neighborhood Center Do you want to take a class but don't have the time? Try a free one-hour class Monday through Friday this week. Learn:

- Art
- Spanish
- Music
- French
- Computers
- Yoga

Classes start at 10:00 a.m. and 2:00 p.m. Go to www.freeclass.cup.org for more information.

B Read the website again. Then answer the questions. Check (✓) the correct events.

Which events . . .	The concert	The food festival	The street fair	The free classes
1. have food?	☐	☑	☑	☐
2. are on Saturday?	☐	☐	☐	☐
3. have a website?	☐	☐	☐	☐
4. are during the day?	☐	☐	☐	☐
5. are at night?	☐	☐	☐	☐
6. are outdoors?	☐	☐	☐	☐

2 Make your own event.

Writing **A** Complete the sentences with the prepositions in the box.

| at | at | at | between | for | ✓from | on | through | to |

1. The event is __*from*__ 6:00 _____ 10:00.
2. The event is _____ 8:00 p.m. _____ the stadium _____ Main Street.
3. Go to www.eventinfo.cup.org _____ more information, or call Jim _____ 555-7777.
4. Call _____ 12:00 p.m. and 5:00 p.m., Monday _____ Friday.

B Imagine you are planning an event. Answer the questions. Use the ideas in the boxes and your own ideas.

Events:	Places:
a play, an art exhibit, a concert, a sports event	the library, the museum, the park, the theater

1. What is the event? _____
2. When and where is it? _____
3. What time does it start and finish? _____
4. What's the cost of the event? Is it free? _____
5. What things are there to do at the event? _____
6. Where or how do people get more information? _____

C Write an ad for an event in your town or city. Give the event a name.

_____
_____
_____

Unit 6 Progress chart

What can you do? Mark the boxes. ☑ = I can . . . ? = I need to review how to . . .	To review, go back to these pages in the Student's Book.
Grammar	
☐ use *There's* and *There are* with singular and plural nouns.	54 and 55
☐ use quantifiers *a lot of*, *some*, *a couple of*, and *no*.	54 and 55
☐ use adjectives before nouns.	55
☐ ask and answer questions about time.	56 and 57
☐ make suggestions with *Let's*.	57
Vocabulary	
☐ name at least 6 adjectives to describe places.	54 and 55
☐ name at least 10 words for neighborhood places.	54 and 55
☐ give times for events.	56 and 57
Conversation strategies	
☐ answer *Me too* or *Me neither* to show I'm like someone.	58 and 59
☐ answer *Right* or *I know* to agree.	59
Writing	
☐ use prepositions *at*, *from*, *in*, *on*, and *to* with times, places, and days.	61

Out and about

Lesson A / Away for the weekend

What's the weather like?

Vocabulary **A** Write two sentences about each picture.

1. _It's hot._
   It's sunny.

2. _____

3. _____

4. _____

5. _____

6. _____

B Answer the questions. Write true answers.

1. How many seasons do you have in your city? What are they? _____

   _____

2. What's your favorite season? Why? _____

   _____

3. What kind of weather do you like? Cold weather? Hot weather? _____

   _____

4. What's the weather like today? Is it warm? _____

   _____

5. What's the weather usually like at this time of year? _____

   _____

6. Does it ever snow in your city? If yes, when? _____

   _____

2 I'm waiting for a friend.

Grammar | Complete the conversation. Use the present continuous.

Erin Hi, Ken. It's Erin. Where are you?

Ken Oh, hi, Erin. I'm at the beach. I _'m spending_ (spend)
the day with Tom. It's beautiful here today! It's, uh . . .

Erin Nice. . . . I'm so happy you _____ (have) fun.

Ken Yeah. We _____ (relax).
We _____ (not do) anything
special – I mean, I _____ (read)
a book, and Tom _____ (swim).
How about you? Are you at work?

Erin No. I _____ (not work) today.

Ken Oh, right. So, where – oops! Uh, I'm sorry.
I _____ (eat) ice cream. I'm starving.

Erin Yeah, me too. I _____ (eat) a cookie.

Ken Really? So, where are you? I mean, are you at home?

Erin No, I'm at Pierre's Café. I _____ (wait)
for a friend. He's very late.

Ken Oh, really? Who?

Erin You!

3 About you

Grammar
and
vocabulary | Are these sentences true or false for you right now? Write *T* (true) or *F* (false).
Then correct the false sentences.

1. __F__ I'm eating dinner right now.
    I'm not eating dinner right now. I'm doing my homework.

2. ____ I'm using a computer.
    _____

3. ____ My family is watching TV.
    _____

4. ____ My friends are working.
    _____

5. ____ It's snowing.
    _____

6. ____ My best friend is skiing.
    _____

1 All about sports

Vocabulary | **A** Write the names of the sports or kinds of exercise under the pictures.

1. _____volleyball_____

2. _____

3. _____

4. _____

5. _____

6. _____

7. _____

8. _____

9. _____

B Complete the chart with the words in part A.

People play . . .	People do . . .	People go . . .
volleyball		

C Answer the questions. Write true answers.

1. What sports do you play? How often? _I play volleyball on Wednesdays and_
   basketball on the weekends.

2. What sports do your friends play? _____
   _____

3. Do you ever go biking? _____
   _____

4. What sports do people in your country like? _____
   _____

❷ What are you doing?

Grammar | **Complete the conversations with present continuous questions.**

1. Joe   Hey, Luis! _What are you doing_____ (What / you / do) ?
   Are you at home?

   Luis   No, I'm at the park. I'm playing tennis.

   Joe   Really? _____ (you / play)
   with Janet?

   Luis   No, I'm playing with John today.

   Joe   Oh. So, _____ (you / have / fun) ?

   Luis   No, I'm not. You know, it's raining here, and it's cold.

   Joe   That's too bad. _____ (you / play)
   right now? In the rain?

   Luis   Yes, we are. And it's my turn to serve. Hold on a minute. . . .

   Joe   So, um, _____ (you / win) ?

   Luis   Uh, no. I'm not playing very well today.

   Joe   Is it because you're talking on your
   cell phone?

2. Janet   Hi, Kelly. _____ (How / you / do) ?

   Kelly   Hi. Great. How are you? _____ (you / work)
   this summer?

   Janet   Yes, I'm working at a gym. I'm teaching there. It's fun.

   Kelly   Really? _____ (What / you / teach) ?

   Janet   Aerobics.

   Kelly   Cool. So, _____ (you / do) other things?
   I mean, _____ (you / swim), too?

   Janet   Yeah. There's a pool at the gym. So, _____
   (you / do) anything special this summer?

   Kelly   Well, no. I'm living in my sister's apartment. She's in
   San Francisco this summer.

   Janet   Really? _____ (What / she / do)
   there?

   Kelly   She's working in a restaurant.

   Janet   _____ (she / meet) a lot of
   new people?

   Kelly   Oh, yes. She's having a good time.

1 Keep the conversation going!

Conversation
strategies Complete the conversation with the follow-up questions in the box.

Where are you working?	✓What are you doing?
Are you practicing your languages?	So, why are you studying Spanish and Portuguese?
What classes are you taking?	Are you enjoying your classes?

Alex   Hey, Kate. How's it going?

Kate   Good. How are things with you?

Alex   Great. But I'm really busy this summer.

Kate   Really? _What are you doing?_

Alex   Well, I'm taking a couple of classes, and I'm working.

Kate   Wow! You're working and studying? _____

Alex   I'm taking Spanish and Portuguese.

Kate   That's interesting. _____

Alex   Yeah, I really am. I'm learning a lot!

Kate   That's great. _____

Alex   Well, I'm thinking about a trip to South America.

Kate   That's exciting!

Alex   Yeah, and that's why I'm working two jobs, you know.

Kate   Right. _____

Alex   Well, I'm working at a Peruvian restaurant from 11:00 to 5:00, and I'm working at a Brazilian music club at night.

Kate   Really? Wow! _____

Alex   Yes, I am! I'm speaking Spanish all day and Portuguese all night.

Kate   That's really cool! But when do you sleep?

Alex   That's a problem. Sometimes I sleep in class.

Kate   Oh, right. That *is* a problem.

2 Asking follow-up questions

Conversation
strategies Complete two follow-up questions for each comment.

1. "I don't play sports, but I often go running with a friend."

Really? Where _do you go running_ ?
How often _____ ?

2. "My parents are on vacation this month."

That's nice. Where _____ ?
Are they _____ ?

3. "My grandparents are visiting this week."

Really? Where _____ ?
How often _____ ?

4. "I'm working nights this summer."

Really? Where _____ ?
What time _____ ?

3 Oh, that's good.

Conversation
strategies Read these people's comments about their summer activities. Complete the responses. Then ask follow-up questions.

1. I'm really enjoying my vacation this summer.

Oh, that's _good_ .
What are you doing ?

2. I'm not doing anything exciting. I'm just reading a lot.

That's _____ .
_____ ?

3. I'm not enjoying this summer at all. I'm working ten hours a day.

Really? That's _____ .
_____ ?

4. I'm just relaxing, and I'm watching a lot of TV.

Hey, that's _____ .
_____ ?

5. I'm exercising a lot at the gym this summer.

That's _____ .
_____ ?

6. What vacation? I'm painting my house right now.

Really? That's _____ .
_____ ?

1 An advice column

Reading | **A** Which sports and exercises do you do? Check (✓) the boxes.

☐ aerobics   ☐ biking   ☐ skiing   ☐ volleyball
☐ basketball   ☐ running   ☐ soccer   ☐ weight training

B Read the advice column. Match the problems with the Sports Professional's advice.

FITNESS TALK

Do you have a question about exercise? Write to Steven, the Sports Professional, for help and good advice.

1. John: I never exercise. I drive to work, and I sit all day. I hate sports, and I don't like the gym. I know it's a good idea to exercise, but how do I start?

_____

2. Amy: I'm really busy this year. I'm going to school, and I'm working part-time at night. I like exercise, but I don't have a lot of time. Help! _____

3. Bill: I do weight training at the gym every day. I usually love exercise, but these days, it's boring. I think I need a break. What do you think?

a. The Sports Professional: Slowly add exercise to your weekly routine. Walk or ride a bike to work – don't drive. Use the stairs, not the elevator. Clean the house, or do the laundry. Just do something – and start today!

b. The Sports Professional: You're right. You need a break. Try exergaming for a change. There are a lot of different types of activities, and each one helps your body in a different way. Don't stop your weight training, and remember, running is always good for you, too.

c. The Sports Professional: Yes, I know the problem, but try and make time. Experts say we need 30 minutes of exercise five times a week. So, do aerobics for 15 minutes in the morning. Go to school. Then go running for 15 minutes in the evening after work.

C Read the advice column again. Then answer the questions.

1. Is John getting enough exercise these days? _____

2. Does John like sports? _____

3. Amy is busy this year. What is she doing? _____

4. What is Amy's problem? _____

5. How often does Bill go to the gym? _____

6. What does Bill do at the gym? _____

2 Write your own advice.

Writing **A** Look again at the advice column on page 56. Find two imperatives the Sports Professional uses in each piece of advice.

Try exergaming for a change.

B Make imperatives for advice. Match the verbs with the words and expressions.

(Don't)	be buy do drive exercise watch	aerobics in the morning at least five times a week shy some good running shoes to work TV all the time	*Don't be shy.* *Buy some good running shoes.* _____ _____ _____ _____

C Read the problems. Reply to each person. Give two pieces of advice using imperatives. Use the ideas above or your own ideas.

1. **Joe:** I watch sports on TV all the time. I'm watching the Olympics this month. It's great, but I don't do any sports. What sports are fun?
   The Sports Professional: *Try a lot of different sports. I like volleyball, tennis, and swimming. Also,* _____

2. **Anita:** This fall, we're playing soccer at school. I'm not enjoying it very much, especially when it's cold! Also, I'm not very good. Help!
   The Sports Professional: _____
   _____

3. **David:** I like exercise, but I'm lazy! I usually exercise for two or three weeks, but then I need a break. Do you have any advice?
   The Sports Professional: _____
   _____

Unit 7 Progress chart

What can you do? Mark the boxes. ☑ = I can . . . ? = I need to review how to . . .	To review, go back to these pages in the Student's Book.
Grammar □ make present continuous statements. □ ask present continuous questions.	66 and 67 68 and 69
Vocabulary □ name at least 6 words to talk about the weather. □ name at least 10 sports and kinds of exercise.	65, 66, and 67 67 and 68
Conversation strategies □ ask follow-up questions to keep the conversation going. □ react to things people say with *That's . . .* expressions.	70 and 71 71
Writing □ use imperatives to give instructions and advice.	73

1　Do a crossword puzzle.

Vocabulary **A**　Complete the crossword puzzle. Write the names of the clothes.

Down

1.

3.

5.

7.

8.

10.

11.

The puzzle shows 2. across filled in: h i g h h e e l s

Across

2.

4.

6.

9.

11.

12.

B　Now find the five highlighted letters in the puzzle. What do they spell?

____ ____ ____ ____ _s_

2 I want to spend some money!

Grammar Complete the conversations with the correct form of the verbs.

1. Mia   Let's go shopping. I _need to buy_ (need / buy) some new clothes.

    Rick   OK. Where do you _____ (want / go) ?

    Mia   To the mall. I _____ (need / get)
    some new jeans. And I _____ (have / get)
    a couple of new suits for work.

    Rick   Listen. You go. I think I _____ (want / stay)
    home. I _____ (not need / buy) anything,
    and I _____ (want / check) my email.

    Mia   OK!

2. Will   I have a date with Megan tonight. She _____ (want / go)
    to an expensive restaurant.

    Ana   Really? Do you have any good clothes?
    Those old jeans are terrible. And you know Megan –
    she _____ (like / wear) designer clothes.

    Will   I know, but I _____ (like / wear) my jeans!
    And I _____ (not want / go) to a
    restaurant anyway. I _____ (want / go) to a movie.

    Ana   Oh, there's the phone. Hello? . . . Will, it's Megan. She's sick.

    Will   Oh, no! Well, now I _____ (not have / change) my clothes!

3 About you

Grammar
and
vocabulary Unscramble the questions. Then write true answers.

1. A to the movies / do / like / What / to / wear / you ? _What do you like to wear to the movies?_
    B _____

2. A nice / have / When / do / to / clothes / you / wear ? _____
    B _____

3. A you / Do / a / have / uniform / to / wear ? _____
    B _____

4. A buy / Do / like / you / to / online / things ? _____
    B _____

5. A clothes / do / What / want / you / buy / to ? _____
    B _____

6. A do / go / like / Where / you / to / shopping ? _____
    B _____

1 Accessories

Vocabulary | Write the words under the pictures using *a* or *some*.

 1. __some jeans__   2. __a dress__   3. _____   4. _____

 5. _____    6. _____    7. _____   8. _____

 9. _____   10. _____    11. _____   12. _____

 13. _____    14. _____   15. _____    16. _____

2 Colors

Vocabulary | Complete the color words in the box. Then answer the questions, and complete the chart. Write three colors to answer each question, if possible.

r_e_d   y_____ w   b_____ k   p_____ e   w_____ e
o_____ e   b_____ e   g_____ n   b_____ n   g_____ y

What colors . . .			
do you like to wear?	blue		
are you wearing right now?			
do you never wear?			
are in your home?			
are your favorites?			
are popular right now?			
are in your country's flag?			

3 How much is this?

Grammar **A** Complete the conversations. Use *this, that, these,* or *those.*

1. Lena Um, excuse me. How much is ___*that*___ dress?
   Clerk The red dress? It's $325.
   Lena Oh. And how about _____ shoes?
   Clerk They're $149.
   Lena Oh, really. And what about _____ T-shirts? Are they expensive, too?
   Clerk They're $49.
   Lena Oh, well. Thanks anyway.

2. Tito Excuse me.
   Seller Yes?
   Tito How much are _____ umbrellas?
   Seller They're $19.99.
   Tito $19.99? Really?
   Seller Oh, wait. Sorry. _____ umbrella is $4.99. _____ umbrellas over here are $19.99.
   Tito OK, so I want _____ umbrella, please.

B Look at the pictures. Write questions and answers.

1.

$99.99

A *How much are those boots?*
B _____

2.

$38

A _____
B _____

3.

$40

A _____
B _____

4.
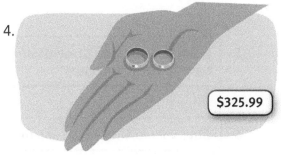
$325.99

A _____
B _____

1 Um, uh, oh!

Conversation strategies | Complete the chart with the "conversation sounds" and expressions in the box.

✓I know.	Let's see.	Really?	Uh,	Um,	Yeah.
Let me think.	Oh.	Right.	Uh-huh.	Well,	

You want to show you agree.	You are surprised.	You need time to think.
I know.		

2 About you

Conversation strategies | Answer the questions with true information. Start each answer with a "time to think" expression.

1. What's your favorite color?

   Let me think. . . . I guess it's green. _____

2. What's your favorite thing to wear?

   _____
   _____

3. How often do you shop online?

   _____
   _____

4. How much do jeans cost these days?

   _____
   _____

5. How many birthday presents do you have to buy this month?

   _____
   _____

6. Does your family like to shop for clothes together?

   _____
   _____

3 Are you listening?

Complete the conversation with the correct expressions.

Roberto	Mom, I have to get some things for college.
Mother	_____*Uh-huh.*_____ What do you need to get? (Uh-huh. / Let me think.)
Roberto	_____ . . . I need to get a new computer and . . . (Um, let's see. / Really!)
Mother	_____ They're expensive. (Let me think. / Oh, really?)
Roberto	I know. But I have to go online a lot for my classes.
Mother	Well, OK. And what else do you want?
Roberto	_____ I want to get a new cell phone and . . . (Uh-huh. / Uh, well . . .)
Mother	_____ I'm surprised. I mean, (Oh, / Um,) you usually don't call, so . . .
Roberto	Well, I text sometimes. Anyway, _____ Oh, yes, and (let's see. / uh-huh.) I have to get some new sneakers.
Mother	_____ You really need new sneakers. Those sneakers are really old. (Let me think. / Uh-huh.)
Roberto	And what else? _____ What else do I need to get? (Oh, really? / Uh, let's see.)
Mother	Well, there's one more thing you need to get . . .
Roberto	What's that?
Mother	A job! You need to pay for these things!

1 Online shopping

Reading **A** Read the article. Who likes to shop online? Who doesn't like to shop online? Check (✓) the correct boxes.

	Likes to shop online	Doesn't like to shop online
Sarah	☐	☐
Matt	☐	☐
Kevin	☐	☐
Susana	☐	☐

Do you like to shop online?

These days *everything* is for sale online – from movie tickets and food, to cars and houses. More and more people download music, movies, magazines, and books. It's easy and convenient. But not *everyone* likes to shop online.

Sarah Cho

"I never shop on the Internet because I like to pay cash. I don't have a credit card, and I don't want to get one. Also, I don't like to spend a lot of time online. I guess I'm not a big fan of shopping."

Matt Carson

"I work long hours – from 9:00 in the morning to 9:00 or 10:00 at night. A lot of stores close at 9:00. But the Internet never closes. I mean, I often shop at 1:00 in the morning. And the prices online are usually really cheap."

Kevin Parker

"There isn't a shopping center near my house. I have to drive an hour to the mall. Online shopping is very convenient. I buy movies, books, clothes, and food online. I never need to go out to a store."

Susana Rivera

"I like to shop with friends. We get up early and go to the mall together. We have a great time. We have lunch and look at the clothes together. When you shop online, you don't spend time with friends. You're alone."

B Read the article again. Then write *Sarah*, *Matt*, *Kevin*, or *Susana* next to the statements.

1. "I don't like to shop online or in stores!" _____*Sarah*_____

2. "I like to shop online because I never have to leave my home." _____

3. "I like to shop online because the prices aren't expensive." _____

4. "I don't like to shop online because I like to go to the mall with friends." _____

5. "I like to shop online because I don't have time during the day." _____

6. "I don't like to shop online because I don't like to go on the Internet." _____

2 What do you think?

Writing **A** Why do people like to shop online? Why do people hate to shop online? Check (✓) the correct box.

I like to shop online . . .	I hate to shop online . . .	Reasons
☐	☐	because I always buy things I don't need.
☐	☐	because it's easy to compare prices.
☐	☐	because it's convenient.
☐	☐	because you don't always have to pay sales tax.
☐	☐	because I often get "spam" emails from shopping websites.

B Answer these questions. Try to write more than *Yes* or *No*.

1. Do you live near a mall or shopping center? _____

2. Do you have time to shop during the week? _____

3. Do you like to go online? _____

4. Do you use a credit card? _____

C Write a short paragraph. Use your ideas from part B, and give reasons. Start like this:
I like to shop online because . . . **or** *I don't like to shop online because . . .*

_____
_____
_____
_____

Unit 8 Progress chart

What can you do? Mark the boxes. ✓ = I can . . . ? = I need to review how to . . .	To review, go back to these pages in the Student's Book.
Grammar ☐ use *like to*, *want to*, *need to*, and *have to* with other verbs.	76 and 77
☐ ask questions with *How much . . . ?*	78 and 79
☐ use *this*, *these*, *that*, and *those*.	79
Vocabulary ☐ name at least 12 kinds of clothes.	75, 76, and 77
☐ name at least 12 accessories.	78 and 79
☐ name at least 8 color words.	78
Conversation strategies ☐ use "time to think" expressions like *Um, . . .* and *Let's see . . . .*	80
☐ use *Uh-huh* and *Oh,* to show that I agree or I'm surprised.	81
Writing ☐ use *because* to give reasons.	83

A wide world

Lesson A / Sightseeing

1 Take a tour!

Vocabulary **A** Complete these suggestions for tourists.

1. In South Korea, visit
   an island .

2. In New York, take pictures
   from a _____ .

3. In Germany, visit an old
   _____ .

4. See a _____ of a
   famous writer in Paris.

5. In Rio de Janeiro, spend a
   day at the _____ .

6. In Egypt, walk around the
   _____ .

7. In London, see a famous
   _____ .

8. Go up a _____ and
   get a good view of Tokyo.

9. Take a _____ of the
   city in Sydney.

Grammar
and
vocabulary **B** Can you do any of the things in part A in your city or town? Write true sentences.

1. _In my area, you can visit an island._ **or** _In my area, you can't visit an island._
2. _____
3. _____
4. _____
5. _____
6. _____
7. _____
8. _____
9. _____

2 What can you do in Toronto?

Grammar | **A** Read the guidebook. What can you do in Toronto? Complete the chart below.

TORONTO, CANADA

1. The CN Tower
Get a good view of the city from 553 meters (1,814 feet). A restaurant, shops, and a glass floor!
Hours: 10:00 a.m. to 11:00 p.m.

2. Casa Loma
Toronto's only castle. Call for a tour.
Open 9:30 a.m. to 5:00 p.m. (Last entry at 4:00 p.m.)

3. Yorkville
Walk around a lively historic neighborhood! Outdoor cafés, shops, and movie theaters.

4. The Art Gallery of Ontario
Hours: 10:00 a.m. to 5:30 p.m.

5. Centre Island
Take the ferry to Centre Island. Enjoy beautiful parks, great restaurants, and a children's amusement park.
Open all day.

6. Harbourfront Centre
Right on Lake Ontario, this huge center has everything for all the family. Ice skating, art, cafés, a music garden, shops, sailing, and boat tours. In the summer, there are outdoor concerts, a market, and special events.
Open from 10:00 a.m. to 9:00 p.m.

On a rainy day	On a sunny day	In the evening	With children
You can go to the Art Gallery of Ontario.			

B Complete the conversations with *can* or *can't*.

1. Jill   What ____*can*____ you do at Harbourfront Centre?

   Dan   Let's see . . . you _____ rent a boat. And at night, you _____ go to an outdoor concert.

   Jill   Sounds great! _____ we go right now?

   Dan   No, we _____ . It opens at 10:00 a.m., and it's only 7:30 a.m. now. It's really early.

   Jill   Oh, you're right. Well, _____ we go to a café for breakfast?

   Dan   Yes, we _____ do that. Let's go!

2. Yoshi   I'm tired today. I don't want to go on another walking tour! Where _____ we go to relax?

   Keiko   Let's go to Yorkville. We _____ have a nice lunch and see a movie.

   Yoshi   OK, but we _____ spend a lot of money. We need to save our money for shopping!

67

1 What countries do you know?

Vocabulary **A** Complete the names of the countries. Then write the countries in the chart below.

1. S _p_ ai _n_
2. ____ ____ str ____ l ____ ____
3. ____ or ____ cc ____
4. C ____ st ____ ____ ic ____
5. R ____ ss ____ ____
6. M ____ x ____ c ____

7. P ____ r ____
8. Fr ____ nc ____
9. S ____ ____ th
   K ____ r ____ ____
10. Ch ____ n ____
11. Th ____ ____ l ____ nd

12. I ____ d ____ ____
13. J ____ p ____ n
14. C ____ n ____ d ____
15. Br ____ z ____ l

I know a lot about . . .			
I don't know a lot about . . .			
They speak English in . . .			
I love the food from . . .			
I don't want to go to . . .			

B Look at the pictures. What kinds of food are these dishes? Write the nationalities.

1. _____ _Japanese_ _____

2. _____

3. _____

4. _____

C Complete the chart.

Food I like	Food I don't like	Food I want to try	Food I can cook
Korean			_French_

2 Where in the world?

Vocabulary | Complete the crossword puzzle.

Across

2. There are no cities in this cold, icy region.

6. This country is in both Europe and Asia.

7. This large region includes Japan and South Korea.

9. Beijing, Shanghai, and Hong Kong are in this country.

10. This long, thin country is in South America.

Crossword (2 across): A N T A R C T I C A

Down

1. They speak both French and English in this North American country.

3. They speak this language in Turkey.

4. Rome, Venice, and Milan are cities in this European country.

5. This large country is in Oceania.

8. They speak this language in Thailand.

3 About you

Grammar | Unscramble the questions. Then write true answers.

1. can / sports / play / What / your best friend ?
   A *What sports can your best friend play?*
   B _____

2. food / mother / make / Can / Mexican / your ?
   A _____
   B _____

3. speak / you / languages / can / What ?
   A _____
   B _____

4. your / speak / English / parents / Can ?
   A _____
   B _____

1 What's this? What are these?

Conversation strategies | What are the things in the pictures? Write sentences. Use the words in the box.

candy   dress   drink   ✓ musical instrument   sandwich   shoe

1. _It's a kind of musical_
   instrument.
   It's called an erhu.

2. _They're a kind of_
   They're called
   _____

3. _____
   _____
   _____

4. _____
   _____
   _____

5. _____
   _____
   _____

6. _____
   _____
   _____

70

2 What's an *Inukshuk*?

Conversation strategies | Complete the sentences. Then unscramble the letters from the boxes to find the answer to the question.

1. A sneaker is a kind of $\boxed{s}$ __h__ __o__ __e__ .
2. A *tortilla* is kind of like a __p__ ___ ___ ___ $\boxed{a}$ ___ ___ .
3. A *balalaika* is like a __g__ ___ ___ $\boxed{t}$ ___ ___ .
4. *Gazpacho* is a kind of tomato __s__ ___ $\boxed{}$ __p__ .
5. *Lassi* is kind of like a ___ ___ ___ __k__ __s__ ___ ___ ___ $\boxed{e}$.
6. Volleyball is a kind of ___ __p__ ___ __r__ $\boxed{}$.

What's an *Inukshuk*?

It's like a __s__ ___ ___ __t__ ___ __e__ . You can see them in Alaska and Greenland.

3 It's a kind of pot.

Conversation strategies | Complete the conversations. Use *like*, *kind of like*, or *a kind of*.

1. A That's a beautiful dish!

    B Thanks. Actually, it's _a kind of_____ pot. It's Japanese.

    A Can you cook with it? It looks so pretty.

    B Yeah! You can make Japanese food _____
       yosenabe in it.

    A Like what?

    B Yosenabe. It's _____ soup.

2. A What can you buy at the market?

    B Well, you can buy food from different countries, things
       _____ fruit. You can buy durians . . .

    A What's a durian?

    B It's _____ fruit.

    A Really?

    B Yeah. It's _____ a melon.

    A Is it good?

    B Yes, I love it.

1 FAQs about Paris

Reading **A** Read the website. Write the correct question heading for each paragraph.

Where can you eat in Paris? ✓What are great places to visit in Paris?
What do people wear in Paris? How can I travel around Paris?

`http://www.parispage...` 🔍

THE PARIS PAGE

Find out all you need to know about Paris! You can send your questions here for other travelers to answer. Or share your information about your trip to Paris.

Frequently Asked Questions (FAQs)

What are great places to visit in Paris?

You have to see the Eiffel Tower on your first visit. Then go to the Louvre. It's a very large and famous art museum. There are also beautiful gardens near it. After that, you can visit the Latin Quarter. It's a very old neighborhood. It has a lot of historic buildings, museums, and great shopping. More

It's easy to travel in Paris. There are trains, buses, and subways. Try the subway system, called the Metro. There are 301 Metro stations in the city. Every building in Paris is near a Metro station, so it's very convenient, too! More

Parisians love food. There are amazing cafés, bistros, and other kinds of restaurants everywhere in the city. You can relax at an outdoor café all day. Cafés open early in the morning and usually close late in the evening. More

Parisians like to "dress up" and wear designer clothes. They don't usually wear shorts, sneakers, or T-shirts to restaurants or concerts. You can wear casual clothes and shoes in Paris, but try to look nice. More

Next

B Read the website again. Then write *T* (true) or *F* (false) for each sentence. Correct the false sentences.

1. The Louvre is a famous garden in Paris. _F_ *The Louvre is a famous art museum in Paris.*

2. The Latin Quarter is a historic building. _____ _____

3. The Metro is a museum in Paris. _____ _____

4. A bistro is a kind of restaurant. _____ _____

5. Cafés open late in Paris. _____ _____

6. Parisians like to wear casual clothes when they go out. _____ _____

2 FAQs about your country

Writing **A** Complete each sentence with three things about your city or country.
Make lists and use commas.

1. _El Salvador_ is famous for _its beautiful beaches, outdoor markets, and great food_ .

2. _____ is famous for _____ .

3. There are great places to see. You can visit _____ .

4. The people usually wear _____ .

B Imagine you are looking at a travel website about your country or city.
Write answers to these questions.

> TRAVEL
>
> 1. I often travel there on business, but I don't usually have a lot of time. Where can I go and
>   what can I see in one day?
>
>   _____
>
>   _____
>
>   _____
>
> 2. I want to visit this summer, but I don't have a lot of money. What can I do for free?
>
>   _____
>
>   _____
>
>   _____
>
> 3. Where can I meet local people? What traditional things can I see or do?
>
>   _____
>
>   _____
>
>   _____

Unit 9 Progress chart

What can you do? Mark the boxes. ✓ = I can . . . ? = I need to review how to . . .	To review, go back to these pages in the Student's Book.
Grammar ☐ use *can* and *can't* to talk about things to do in a city.	86 and 87
☐ use *can* and *can't* to talk about ability.	88 and 89
Vocabulary ☐ use at least 10 new sightseeing words.	86 and 87
☐ name at least 15 countries and 5 regions.	88
☐ name at least 10 nationalities and 10 languages.	88 and 89
Conversation strategies ☐ use *a kind of* and *kind of like* to explain new words.	90
☐ use *like* to give examples.	91
Writing ☐ use commas to separate items in a list.	93

1 What did they do last night?

Grammar **What did these people do last night? What didn't they do? Complete two sentences for each picture. Use the simple past.**

stay home / visit her parents

1. Kate _stayed home_ .
   She _didn't visit her parents_ .

watch TV / practice her guitar

2. Rita _____ .
   She _____ .

study English / cook dinner

3. Mee-Sun _____ .
   She _____ .

play chess / watch a movie

4. Ali and Sam _____ .
   They _____ .

listen to music / email friends

5. Emil _____ .
   He _____ .

invite friends over / clean the house

6. Joe and Ken _____ .
   They _____ .

2 How was your weekend?

Grammar | Complete Grace's email. Use the simple past.

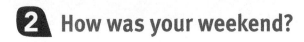

New Message ⬛ ⬜ ✕

To: Paulina Lopez
From: Grace Chen
Subject: How was your weekend?

Hi Paulina!

I really _enjoyed_ (enjoy) the weekend! I _____ (invite) a friend
over on Saturday. She's my co-worker, and she's very nice. We
_____ (play) tennis in the morning and _____ (stay) at the
tennis club for lunch. Then we _____ (practice) yoga and
_____ (walk) in the park.

In the evening, we _____ (watch) a movie and _____ (cook)
a big dinner. We _____ (talk) a lot, but we _____ (not talk)
about work. And we _____ (not watch) TV all day – a nice change!

Then on Sunday, I _____ (study) English and _____ (clean) the
house. Hey! You _____ (not call) me on Sunday! Call me soon, OK?
Tell me about your weekend.

Grace

3 About you

Grammar
and
vocabulary | Write true sentences about your weekend. Use the simple past. Add more information.

1. invite a friend over   _I invited a friend over for dinner._ **or** _I didn't invite a friend over for dinner._

2. stay home   _____

3. study for an exam   _____

4. clean the house   _____

5. call a friend   _____

6. check my email   _____

7. chat online   _____

8. practice my English   _____

9. listen to music   _____

10. rent a car   _____

11. cook a big meal   _____

12. exercise   _____

1 A weekly planner

Grammar and vocabulary | **Read Jenna's planner. Then complete the sentences below. Use the simple past of the verbs in the box.**

SUNDAY	MONDAY	TUESDAY	WEDNESDAY
Movie with Meg 1:00 ✓	Read <u>The Pearl</u> ✓	Write book report on <u>The Pearl</u> ✓	Piano lesson 4:30 ✗
<u>Romeo and Juliet</u> – Grand Theater 2:00 ✗	Read art magazine ✗	Write history paper ✗	Doctor's appointment 2:00 ✓
Homework ✗	Homework ✓	Homework ✓	Homework ✓

THURSDAY	FRIDAY	SATURDAY
Call: Mom ✓ Felipe ✓ Lia ✓	Alison's party 7:30 ✓	Shopping! Need new: shoes ✗
Make dinner 6:30 ✗	Mike 8:00 ✗	jacket ✓
Homework ✓	Homework ✓	Homework ✗

| buy | do | go | have | make | read | ✓see | write |

1. On Sunday, Jenna _____*saw*_____ a movie.
   She _*didn't see*_ a play.

2. On Monday, Jenna _____ a book in English.
   She _____ a magazine.

3. Jenna _____ a book report on Tuesday.
   She _____ a history paper.

4. Jenna _____ a doctor's appointment on Wednesday.
   She _____ a piano lesson this week.

5. On Thursday, Jenna _____ a lot of phone calls.
   She _____ dinner.

6. On Friday, Jenna _____ to a party.
   She _____ out with Mike.

7. Jenna _____ a new jacket on Saturday.
   She _____ new shoes.

8. Jenna _____ homework every school day.
   She _____ homework on the weekend.

2 About you

Grammar and vocabulary

A Complete the questions in the questionnaire. Use the simple past of the verbs in the box. Then write true answers. Write more than *yes* or *no*.

| do | eat | ✓go | have | make | see | speak | take | write |

QUESTIONNAIRE: Did you . . . ?

1. __Did__ you __go__ out a lot last week?
Yes, I did. I went out every night last week. **or** _No, I didn't. I stayed home._ _____

2. _____ you and your family _____ dinner in front of the TV last night?
_____

3. _____ you _____ anything interesting last weekend?
_____

4. _____ you _____ in a restaurant on Friday night?
_____

5. _____ your class _____ a test or an exam last week?
_____

6. _____ you _____ dinner every night last week?
_____

7. _____ your best friend _____ you an email yesterday?
_____

8. _____ your parents _____ a movie on Saturday night?
_____

9. _____ you _____ to a lot of friends in class yesterday?
_____

B Write a sentence about each day last week. Write one thing you did each day.

1. Monday _____
2. Tuesday _____
3. Wednesday _____
4. Thursday _____
5. Friday _____
6. Saturday _____
7. Sunday _____

1 Responding to news

A Complete the conversations. Circle and write the best response.

1. A I bought a new TV today.
   B *Good for you!*

   (a.) Good for you!
   b. I'm sorry to hear that.
   c. Good luck!

2. A I'm 25 today!
   B _____

   a. I'm sorry to hear that.
   b. Good luck!
   c. Happy birthday!

3. A My wife had a baby girl last night.
   B _____

   a. Good for you!
   b. Happy birthday!
   c. Congratulations!

4. A I have a job interview today.
   B _____

   a. I'm sorry to hear that.
   b. Good luck!
   c. Happy birthday!

5. A I finally passed my English exam.
   B _____

   a. Thank goodness!
   b. I'm sorry to hear that.
   c. Good luck!

6. A I didn't get the job I wanted.
   B _____

   a. I'm sorry to hear that.
   b. Thank goodness!
   c. Good for you!

B Your friend tells you some news, and you respond. Write the conversations.

1. Your friend bought a new car, and he got a bargain.

   I bought a new car today. I got a bargain.   *Good for you!*

2. Your friend got 100% on her English exam.

3. Your friend finally got a job.

4. Your friend wanted to go on vacation, but he has no money.

2 You did?

A Complete the conversations with the expressions in the box.

✓You did? You did? You did? Good luck! I'm sorry to hear that. Good for you.

1. Lilly Did you have a busy day?

   Beth Yeah, I'm exhausted. I went shopping downtown.

   Lilly ___You___ ___did?___ Did you buy anything?

   Beth Yes, I bought a new suit. And a blouse and shoes.

   Lilly _____ _____ _____

   Beth And then I had lunch with Maria, and we talked all
   afternoon. How about you?

   Lilly I cleaned the house, did the laundry, and made dinner.

   Beth _____ _____ That's great! I'm starving! Let's eat!

2. Jun Did you have a good week?

   José Actually, no. I had five exams.

   Jun _____ _____ That's awful. Did you pass?

   José Well, I passed three and failed two.

   Jun Oh. _____ _____ _____ _____ _____

   José And I have two exams tomorrow, too.

   Jun _____ _____ Study hard!

B Write two responses for each piece of news.

1. I had a terrible vacation in Hawaii.

   You did? I'm sorry to hear that.

2. I took my driver's test yesterday.

   _____ _____

3. I wrote an article for a magazine last month.

   _____ _____

4. My friend and I worked all weekend.

   _____ _____

1 A busy birthday . . .

Reading **A** Look at the four pictures. Then read Peter's blog. Number the pictures in order from 1 to 4.

Friday, May 28 11:45 p.m.

I had a crazy day today. I had an English exam, and it's my birthday!

I had the exam at 8:30 this morning. I needed to study, so I woke up early – at 6:30 a.m. I took a shower, made some coffee, and studied for about an hour. Well, the coffee didn't work. I fell asleep! I woke up at 8:20 with my head on my books. I had ten minutes before the test started!

I ran outside, got on my bike, and went to English class. I got there right at 8:30, but guess what! The teacher never came! My classmates and I waited about half an hour. Then we left. It's great. Now I can really study for the exam.

I had breakfast, and then I went to my next class – math. ☹ I think math is really hard, but I have to take it. My teacher talked for an hour. I wanted to write some notes, but I fell asleep. I need to borrow my friend's notes.

After I finished class, I met my friend Louisa, and we went to a movie together. It was my birthday, so she paid! Great! We saw a new romantic drama. You know, I usually like drama movies a lot, but I didn't like that movie very much.

When I got home from the movie, my mother called and sang "Happy Birthday" to me. Now I have to stay up and finish a paper for a class tomorrow. I hope I don't fall asleep again!

Posted by Peter Miller

0 comments

B Read the blog again. Then answer the questions. Give reasons for the answers.

1. Did Peter get up late? _No, he didn't. He needed to study._
2. Did Peter take an English exam? _____
3. Did he listen to his math teacher? _____
4. Did he go out with a friend? _____
5. Did Peter's mother call? _____
6. Do you think he's a good student? _____

2 My last birthday

Writing **A Read the blog on page 80 again. Match the two parts of each sentence.**

1. Peter studied when __c__
2. Peter had breakfast after _____
3. When Peter went to his math class, _____
4. Peter finished classes. Then _____
5. Peter saw a movie before _____

a. he went home.
b. he fell asleep again.
✓c. he got up in the morning.
d. he met his friend Louisa.
e. he left his English class.

B Think about a day you remember well. Answer these questions. Write more than *yes* or *no*.

1. Did you work or have classes? _____
2. Did you go out with friends? _____
3. Did you do something fun? _____
4. Did you eat any of your favorite foods? _____
5. Did you go to any stores? _____
6. Did you get home late? _____

**C Write a paragraph for your own blog. Use your ideas from part B.
Use *before*, *after*, *when*, or *then*, if possible.**

I remember my last birthday. I _____
_____
_____
_____
_____

Unit 10 Progress chart

What can you do? Mark the boxes. ☑ = I can . . . ? = I need to review how to . . .	To review, go back to these pages in the Student's Book.
Grammar ☐ make simple past statements with regular verbs.	98 and 99
☐ make simple past statements with irregular verbs.	100 and 101
☐ ask simple past *yes-no* questions.	101
Vocabulary ☐ make simple past forms of at least 12 regular verbs.	98 and 99
☐ make simple past forms of at least 8 irregular verbs.	100 and 101
☐ use time expressions with the simple past.	101
Conversation strategies ☐ use responses like *Good for you!* and *Congratulations!*	102 and 103
☐ use *You did?* to show I'm listening, surprised, or interested.	103
Writing ☐ use *before*, *after*, *when*, and *then* to order events.	105

1 Yesterday

Vocabulary | Complete the sentences. Use the words in the box.

| busy | ✓happy | nervous | nice | quiet | scared |

1. Yesterday was my birthday. My friends had a party for me, and I got a lot of presents. I was very ___happy___ .
2. My family and I live in a very small town. There are no clubs or movie theaters. My town is really _____ – especially at night.
3. I started a new job yesterday. I was really _____ of my new boss.
4. I had a lot of things to do yesterday. I was pretty _____ .
5. My best friend's parents are friendly. They're very _____ .
6. We had a French test last week. I was really _____ , but I passed.

2 It was fun!

Vocabulary | Choose the best two words to complete each sentence. Cross out the wrong word.

I remember my first driving lesson. Before I met the teacher, I was really ~~scary~~ / **nervous** / **scared**. But then I relaxed because he was very **nice** / **strict** / **friendly**. The lesson was **awful** / **good** / **fun** because I didn't make a lot of mistakes. I was pretty good. At the end of the lesson, I was **exhausted** / **lazy** / **tired**. It was hard work! After ten lessons, I took my test, but I didn't pass. I wasn't **awful** / **pleased** / **happy**. But I passed three weeks later. Now I can drive my dad's **nice** / **new** / **awful** car.

3 I remember . . .

Grammar | **Complete the conversations with *was*, *wasn't*, *were*, or *weren't*.**

1. Sally   Do you remember your first date, Grandpa?

   Grandpa   Yes. I ___*was*___ 16, and the girl _____ in my class.

       We _____ classmates. We went to the movies.

   Sally   _____ you nervous?

   Grandpa   No, I _____ . It _____ a lot of fun.

   Sally   Do you remember her name?

   Grandpa   Yes. Grandma!

2. Paula   I remember my first day of high school.

       It _____ a hot day, and I went with

       two of my friends.

   Kenton   _____ you scared?

   Paula   No, we _____ really scared, but I

       guess we _____ a little nervous.

   Kenton   _____ the teachers friendly?

   Paula   Yes, they _____ very nice.

       Thank goodness.

3. Sun-Hee   Do you remember your first college English class?

   Carla   Yes, it _____ last year. I _____ very good at

       English, and I made a lot of mistakes. My partner's

       English _____ very good, so he _____

       very happy with me!

   Sun-Hee   _____ he smart? I mean, intelligent?

   Carla   Yes, he _____ .

   Sun-Hee   So, was your first class fun?

   Carla   No, it _____ . In fact,

       it _____ awful.

1 About you

Grammar and vocabulary
A Unscramble the questions. Then write true answers.

1. trip or vacation / was / last / your / When ?

   A *When was your last trip or vacation?*

   B _____

2. go / did / Where / exactly / you ?

   A _____

   B _____

3. weather / like / was / the / What ?

   A _____

   B _____

4. you / there / do / did / What ?

   A _____

   B _____

5. were / there / How / you / long ?

   A _____

   B _____

Grammar
B Read about Emi's first trip to the park with a friend. Write questions for the answers.

"We weren't very old – I think I was eight, and my friend was ten. We went to the park, but my mother didn't know. We had a great time! We went swimming in the pool. I remember it was a beautiful day – warm and sunny. We were there about an hour. Then we got hungry, so we went home. When we got back, my mother wasn't too happy."

1. A *How old was Emi?*

   B Eight.

2. A _____

   B To the park.

3. A _____

   B Her friend.

4. A _____

   B They went swimming.

5. A _____

   B Warm and sunny.

6. A _____

   B About an hour.

2 *Get* and *go*

Vocabulary **A** Which of these expressions do you use with *get*? Which do you use with *go*? Which can you use with *get* and *go*? Complete the chart.

✓ back	to bed	scared	swimming	to the movies	a view of something
✓ lost	a gift	skiing	(an) autograph	snorkeling	along with someone
home	hiking	camping	on vacation	a bad sunburn	to see a concert / movie
sick	biking	married	up early or late	on a road trip	to the beach

get	go	get and go
lost		back

B Complete the questions with *get* or *go*. Then write your own answers.

1. A What time do you ___*go* **or** *get*___ to bed on weeknights?

   B _____

2. A How often do you _____ swimming?

   B _____

3. A Did you _____ a bad sunburn last year?

   B _____

4. A What did you _____ for your last birthday?

   B _____

5. A Can you think of someone you don't _____ along with?

   B _____

6. A Where do you want to _____ on vacation this year?

   B _____

7. A Do you _____ up early in the morning?

   B _____

1 Asking questions

Conversation strategies
Complete each conversation with two questions.

1.   Sadie   How was your weekend?

       Bill   It was awful. We went hang gliding. I hated it!

     Sadie   That's too bad.

       Bill   Yeah. Anyway, how about you?

               What did you do?

               Did you do anything special?

     Sadie   Well, we rented a car and went camping.

       Bill   That sounds nice.

2.   Dirk   Did you go out last night?

       Leo   Yeah, I met a friend and went to a club.

              _____

              _____

       Dirk   Oh, I went to the laundromat and did my laundry. I didn't do anything exciting.

3.   Shira   I went to the concert last Saturday.

       Jaz   I did, too! The band sounded great.

              _____

              _____

     Shira   Oh, it was fantastic. Well, anyway, it's 11:30.

       Jaz   Yeah, it's late. See you tomorrow.

4. Gabor   So, did you work last weekend?

       Koji   Yeah, Saturday and Sunday. We were really busy.

              _____

              _____

     Gabor   Let's see . . . I went shopping, um, and saw a movie. Then on Sunday, I played tennis, made dinner, . . .

       Koji   I guess you were busy, too!

2 Well, anyway, . . .

A Use *anyway* three times in this conversation. Leave two of the blanks empty.

Mirka   Where were you last week? Were you away?

Arlen   Yes, I was in Mexico on business.

Mirka   Mexico? What was that like?

Arlen   Oh, great. The customers there are really nice.
_____ I always enjoy my trips to Mexico.
The people are so friendly.

Mirka   That's nice. _____ So you're traveling a
lot these days.

Arlen   Yeah. About six times a year. _____ ,
what about you? Did you have a good week?

Mirka   Not bad. I had a lot of meetings – you know, the
usual. _____ , do you want to go out
tonight? We can have dinner maybe.

Arlen   Sure. We can meet after work.

Mirka   OK. Well, _____ , I have to go. See you later.

B Use the instructions to complete the conversations.

1. Friend   What do you usually do on the weekends?

    You   *I usually go out with friends. What about you?*

(Answer. Then ask a question about your friend.)

    Friend   Me? I usually go to see a movie. Sometimes a friend and I go camping or hiking.

2. Friend   I'm enjoying my new job. My boss is OK, and the people are nice. We get
    along – it's a friendly place.

    You   That's nice. _____

(Change the topic. Invite your friend for dinner tomorrow.)

    Friend   Tomorrow? Sounds great. What time? Seven?

3. Friend   What did you do for your last birthday?

    You   _____

(Answer. Then end the conversation. It's late.)

    Friend   OK. Talk to you later.

4. Friend   So how was your weekend?

    You   _____

(Answer. Then change the topic. Invite your friend to do something fun next weekend.)

    Friend   Sure. Sounds like fun.

1 My first job

Reading | **A** Read the story. What are these people like? Match the names with the adjectives.

1. Diana ___a___
2. Joe _____
3. Megan _____
4. Rick _____

✓a. friendly
b. nervous
c. good looking
d. strict

Tell Us About Your First Job

Reader Megan Walker writes in with a story about her first job.

I remember my first job. I worked in an outdoor café one summer. It was called Sunny's. I got free drinks and food. My boss Diana was very friendly, and I got along well with her. Her husband Joe worked there, too, but he was really strict. On my first day, I was late because I got lost on the subway. After that, Joe was never too happy with me.

So, every day I served sandwiches and coffee. The café was really busy all the time. I wasn't a very good server, so I was often nervous. Also, I was always exhausted by the end of the day.

One day, I was really tired, so I asked to go home early. Joe looked angry, but he said, "OK. Fine." I left and went to the subway.

Then I met my friend Rick on the street. He was really good looking, and I liked him a lot. He said, "Do you want to go and eat something?" I said, "Yes. OK. Where?" And he said, "I know a café near here. Let's go there. They have good sandwiches."

So we went back to Sunny's and sat down to eat! We waited for about ten minutes before Joe finally came over to the table. He was very busy, so he didn't look at me. He said, "I'm sorry. One of the servers left early. Are you ready to order?" We stayed for an hour. I was lucky because my boss never saw me, but I had to pay for my sandwich and soda!

– *Megan Walker*
New York City

B Read Megan's story again. Then answer the questions.

1. Where did Megan work? *She worked at Sunny's.* _____

2. How did Megan get to work? _____

3. What kind of food did she serve? _____

4. What was the café like? _____

5. Why did she leave early one day? _____

6. Why did she go back to Sunny's? _____

7. How long did they stay at Sunny's? _____

2 He said, . . .

Writing **A** Read the rest of the story. Rewrite their conversation after they leave the café. Use quoted speech. Add capital letters and correct punctuation (" " , . ?).

Rick and I left the café and talked for a few minutes.

rick asked how did you like the café   _Rick asked, "How did you like the café?"_

I said it's nice _____

he said the service wasn't very good _____

I said well one of the servers left early _____

rick said people are so lazy these days _____

I said yes I know _____

But I didn't tell Rick I was the server!

B Think about a time you met a friend for the first time. Answer these questions.

1. How old were you? _____

2. What was your friend's name? _____

3. How did you first meet? What happened? _____

4. What did you say when you first met? I said, "_____ ."

5. What did your friend say? She / He said, "_____ ."

C Now write a story about meeting your friend. Use your ideas from part B.

_When we met, I was 13 and _____ . _____

_____

_____

_____

Unit 11 Progress chart

What can you do? Mark the boxes. ✓ = I can . . . ? = I need to review how to . . .	To review, go back to these pages in the Student's Book.
Grammar ☐ make simple past statements and questions with *be*.	108 and 109
☐ ask simple past information questions.	110
Vocabulary ☐ name at least 12 words to describe people or experiences.	108 and 109
☐ name at least 4 new expressions with *go*.	111
☐ name at least 5 new expressions with *get*.	111
Conversation strategies ☐ ask and answer questions to show interest.	112
☐ use *Anyway* to change the topic or end a conversation.	113
Writing ☐ use capitals and punctuation in quoted speech.	115

1 Mmmmm!

Vocabulary | **Write the names of the foods. Then find the words in the puzzle. Look in these directions (→ ↓).**

1. _____meat_____

2. _____seafood_____

3. _____

4. _____

5. _____

6. _____

7. _____

8. _____

F	F	V	C	A	R	R	O	T	S
R	X	E	B	I	B	E	E	F	S
U	O	G	A	X	R	M	E	A	T
I	A	E	N	S	E	I	S	T	A
T	E	T	A	E	A	L	L	C	E
G	G	A	N	A	D	K	F	H	P
P	G	B	A	F	R	U	I	E	P
O	S	L	S	O	P	P	D	E	A
T	F	E	N	O	U	D	L	S	S
A	I	S	Z	D	I	H	G	E	T
T	S	H	R	I	C	E	F	Q	A
O	H	C	H	I	C	K	E	N	M
E	C	U	C	U	M	B	E	R	S
S	H	E	L	L	F	I	S	H	Z

9. _____

10. _____

11. _____

12. _____

13. _____

14. _____

15. _____

16. _____

17. _____

18. _____

2 An invitation to dinner

Grammar **A** Read the invitation. Then circle the correct words to complete the emails.

Invitation to *a housewarming party and dinner*
On *Saturday night at 7:00 p.m.*
At *my new apartment!*

Bring a friend. Tell me if you
have food allergies or anything.

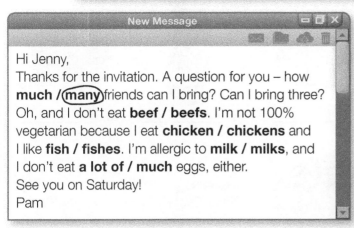

Hi Jenny,
Thanks for the invitation. A question for you – how
much / many friends can I bring? Can I bring three?
Oh, and I don't eat **beef / beefs**. I'm not 100%
vegetarian because I eat **chicken / chickens** and
I like **fish / fishes**. I'm allergic to **milk / milks**, and
I don't eat **a lot of / much** eggs, either.
See you on Saturday!
Pam

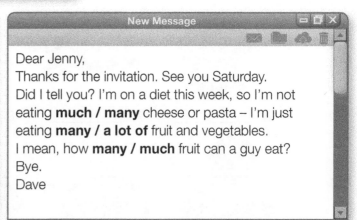

Dear Jenny,
Thanks for the invitation. See you Saturday.
Did I tell you? I'm on a diet this week, so I'm not
eating **much / many** cheese or pasta – I'm just
eating **many / a lot of** fruit and vegetables.
I mean, how **many / much** fruit can a guy eat?
Bye.
Dave

B Write your own email to Jenny. Tell her about these foods.

- food you like
- food you don't like
- food you eat a lot of
- food you don't eat a lot of

New Message

Dear Jenny,
Thanks for the invitation to the party. _____
_____
_____
_____
_____
_____

3 About you

Grammar
and
vocabulary
Complete the questions with *How much* or *How many*. Then write your own answers.

1. *How many* students in your class are vegetarians? _____
2. _____ milk does your family buy every week? _____
3. _____ times a week do you eat chicken? _____
4. _____ shellfish do you eat? Do you eat a lot? _____
5. _____ of your friends are picky eaters? _____
6. _____ cans of soda do you drink a day? _____

1 At the supermarket

Vocabulary | **Write the words under the pictures. Then write the food in the chart below.**

 1. _apples_

 2. _____

 3. _____

 4. _____

 5. _____

 6. _____

 7. _____

 8. _____

 9. _____

 10. _____

 11. _____

 12. _____

 13. _____

 14. _____

 15. _____

 16. _____

 17. _____

 18. _____

 19. _____

 20. _____

meat and seafood	fruit	vegetables	other
	apples		

2 What would you like?

Grammar | **Complete the conversations. Use *would you like* or *'d like*.**

1. Jim   What _would you like_ ?

   Megan   I _____ ice cream, please.

   Jim   _____ chocolate sprinkles?

   Megan   Yes, please.

2. Server   Good evening. _____ something to drink?

   Dan   Oh, just water, please.

   Server   OK. And what _____ to eat?

   Dan   Um, I _____ the salmon, please.

   Server   _____ some green beans with it?

   Dan   Actually, I _____ some spinach, please.

3. Greg   Where _____ to go for dinner?

   Sheila   Oh, I don't know. I _____ to go somewhere around here.

   Greg   _____ to try the new Thai restaurant?

   Sheila   Oh, yes! I _____ something spicy.

3 *Some* or *any*

Grammar | **Complete the conversations with *some* or *any*.**

1. Ming   Polly, try _some_ lamb.

   Polly   Gosh, it's hot! I need _____ water . . . now!

   Ming   Here. Drink _____ soda.

2. John   Do you have _____ chocolate cookies?

   Ken   No, but we have _____ peanut butter cookies.

   John   OK, I'll take _____ .

3. Sara   Would you like _____ potato chips?

   Craig   Yeah, but I don't have _____ money.

   Sara   Oh, and I don't have _____ , either.

A sandwich or something

1 Something for lunch

Conversation strategies **Complete the conversation with *or something* or *or anything*.**

Trish Do you go out for lunch every day or . . . ?

Pete Well, I don't usually eat lunch. I don't like to eat a
big meal _or anything_ at lunchtime.

Trish No? You don't have a snack _____ ?

Pete Well, I sometimes have a hot drink, like hot
chocolate _____ .

Trish Well, I'm hungry – I'd like a sandwich
_____ . Would you like something to eat?

Pete Well, maybe . . .

Trish How about a salad _____ ?

Pete Yes, OK. Actually, I'd like a chicken sandwich.
Oh, let's get some ice cream _____ , too. I guess I *am* hungry!

2 About you

Conversation strategies **Answer the questions. Write true answers. Use *or something* or *or anything*.**

1. Are you a picky eater? *Well, I don't eat fish or shrimp or anything.*

2. What do you usually have for dinner? _____

3. How about lunch? _____

4. What do you like to order in restaurants? _____

5. What do you drink with meals? _____

6. What kinds of snacks do you like? _____

③ Would you like to go out or . . . ?

**Complete the conversations. Which questions can end with *or* . . . ?
Add *or* . . . where possible.**

1. Paul   What would you like for dinner tonight _____ ?
             Would you like to go out <u>*or* . . .</u> ?

    Val   Yes, please! I'd love to eat out.

    Paul   That's great. So can I choose the restaurant _____ ?

    Val   Sure.

    Paul   Let's see . . . would you like a pizza _____ ?

    Val   Um, I don't want Italian tonight. How about an
             Asian place? Do you like Korean or Thai _____ ?

    Paul   Uh, I don't really care for spicy food.

    Val   Let me think . . . do you want to get a hamburger _____ ?

    Paul   Yeah! With maybe some French fries
             and some cookies.

    Val   OK! Stop! I'm starving! Let's go!

2. Kate   It's my birthday today.

    Sally   Happy birthday! Do you have plans _____ ?

    Kate   I had plans, but my friend just called. He's sick.

    Sally   That's terrible! I know. Let's eat at my house. I can
             cook some steaks or something. What do you
             think _____ ?

    Kate   That's very nice, thanks, but I'm a vegetarian.

    Sally   Oh. Do you eat pasta _____ ?

    Kate   Well, I can't eat pasta or anything heavy right
             now. I'm on a diet.

    Sally   OK. No pasta. What would you like _____ ?

    Kate   Do you have any fruit _____ ?

    Sally   Sorry. I ate the last banana this morning
             before I went to work. I have some carrots. . . .

    Kate   Let's stop at the supermarket on our way
             to your house.

1 Healthy fast food

Reading | **A** Read the blog post. Find the answers to these questions.

1. Where did the writer eat breakfast? _____
2. What breakfast food does the writer recommend? _____
3. How many calories were in the writer's lunch? _____

TASTES GOOD, AND GOOD FOR YOU!

We often think of fast food as hamburgers, fried chicken, hot dogs, and French fries. However, some fast-food restaurants are starting to offer healthy foods, too. But how healthy is "healthy" fast-food, and how does it taste? I went to some famous fast-food restaurants last week to find the answer and was pleasantly surprised. Here are the two healthy fast-food choices I recommend.

BURGER RESTAURANTS: OATMEAL, PLEASE!

Many burger restaurants open early and serve breakfast, too. One popular restaurant chain has a breakfast with more than 1,000 calories. That's about half the calories you need for a whole day! For a healthy option, you can now choose apple slices (15 calories), fruit and nuts (210 calories), or oatmeal (290 calories). I tried the oatmeal, and it was delicious!

MEXICAN RESTAURANTS: I'D LIKE IT IN A BOWL

I love Mexican fast food as a special treat, but I'm pleased to see that my favorite taco restaurant now has a lot of healthy choices on the menu. A taco salad with beef and cheese is about 600 calories. However, I went for chicken. You can make your own meal with chicken, rice, tomatoes, and other healthy foods. I tried it for lunch. I got it in a bowl and said no to the tortilla chips. It was very tasty and only 450 calories.

Do you know any great, healthy fast-food places? Tell us in the comments section.

B Read the blog post again. Then choose the correct words to complete these sentences.

1. The writer wanted to try some **hamburgers / healthy food** last week.
2. He thinks that 1,000 calories **is / is not** a lot for breakfast.
3. He **enjoyed / didn't enjoy** the oatmeal.
4. He had **taco salad / chicken** for lunch.
5. He **ate / didn't eat** tortilla chips with his lunch.
6. His lunch was **very / not very** healthy.

2 Restaurant reviews

Writing | **A** Jill Heacock is a restaurant reviewer. She ate at the Seafood Palace last week, and she loved it. Circle the correct words to complete Jill's review.

THIS WEEK'S RESTAURANT: **THE SEAFOOD PALACE**   ★ ★ ★ ★

by Jill Heacock

Last week, I went to the Seafood Palace – it's a **terrible /(wonderful)** restaurant. I loved it. I was there on a busy night, and the atmosphere was **fun / formal**. The food was **awful / delicious**, and every dish came to the table **cold / hot**. I really liked the shrimp. Very tasty! The service was **excellent / slow**, the servers were really **friendly / lazy**, and the meal was **cheap / expensive**. I only spent $12!

The Seafood Palace is a good place to hang out with friends or have dinner with your family. Try it!

B Imagine you are a restaurant reviewer. You ate at a restaurant, and you hated it. Write your review.

THIS WEEK'S RESTAURANT: _____   ★

by _____

Last week, I went to _____ – it's a terrible restaurant! _____

_____

_____

_____

_____

_____

Unit 12 Progress chart

What can you do? Mark the boxes. ✓ = I can . . . ? = I need to review how to . . .	To review, go back to these pages in the Student's Book.
Grammar ☐ use countable and uncountable nouns.	118 and 119
☐ make statements and questions with *much*, *many*, and *a lot of*.	118 and 119
☐ make statements and questions with *some*, *any*, and *not any*.	120 and 121
☐ make offers and requests with *would like*.	121
Vocabulary ☐ name at least 5 categories of food.	118 and 119
☐ name at least 25 different foods.	118, 119, and 120
Conversation strategies ☐ use *or something* and *or anything*.	122
☐ use *or . . . ?* in *yes-no* questions to make them less direct.	123
Writing ☐ use expressions to talk about restaurants.	124 and 125

Illustration credits

Ken Batelman: 42 **Harry Briggs:** 15, 61 *(4 at bottom)*, 69 **Domninic Bugatto:** 8, 23, 27, 38, 59, 78 **Cambridge University Press:** 67
Matt Collins: 22, 54 **Chuck Gonzales:** 5, 11, 26, 45, 80 **Cheryl Hoffman:** 3, 24, 47, 61 *(2 at top)* **Jon Keegan:** 19, 51, 94, 95
Frank Montagna: 2, 13, 21, 53, 82, 83 **Greg White:** 7, 16, 37, 79 **Terry Wong:** 30, 46, 63, 74, 86 **Filip Yip:** 70

Photo credits

3 *(clockwise from top left)* ©Exactostock/SuperStock; ©Elea Dumas/Getty Images; ©MIXA/Getty Images; ©Thinkstock 4 ©Ryan McVay/Getty Images 7 ©wavebreakmedia/Shutterstock 10 *(clockwise from top left)* ©Andresr/Shutterstock; ©MTPA Stock/Masterfile; ©Spencer Grant/PhotoEdit; ©Jose Luiz Pelaez Inc./Corbis; ©Medioimages/Photodisc/Thinkstock; ©Terry Doyle/Getty Images 11 *(top to bottom)* ©Image Source/SuperStock; ©kurhan/Shutterstock 12 *(pen)* ©Phant/Shutterstock; *(potato chips)* ©Thinkstock; *(wallet)* ©AlexTois/Shutterstock; *(laptop)* ©Alex Staroseltsev/Shutterstock; *(umbrella)* ©K. Miri Photography/Shutterstock; *(bag)* ©Hemera Technologies/Thinkstock; *(glasses)* ©Ingvar Bjork/Shutterstock; *(keys)* ©SELEZNEV VALERY/Shutterstock; *(notebook)* ©zirconicusso/Shutterstock; *(smartphone)* ©Oleksiy Mark/Shutterstock; *(water bottle)* ©lucadp/Shutterstock; *(eraser)* ©GreenStockCreative/Shutterstock; *(watch)* ©Venus Angel/Shutterstock; ©Butterfly Hunter/Shutterstock; *(pencil)* ©Julia Ivantsova/Shutterstock; *(hand holding smartphone)* ©Thinkstock; *(hand holding water bottle)* ©DenisNata/Shutterstock; *(all others)* ©George Kerrigan 14 *(top row, left to right)* ©Rtimages/Shutterstock; ©Cambridge University Press; ©Thinkstock; ©Cambridge University Press *(middle row, left to right)* ©Ryan McVay/Thinkstock; ©Ryan McVay/Thinkstock; ©Thinkstock; ©Pixtal/age Fotostock *(bottom row, left to right)* ©Cambridge University Press; ©Cambridge University Press; ©Photodisc/Thinkstock; ©vovan/Shutterstock 19 ©Design Pics/SuperStock 20 *(clockwise from top left)* ©Exactostock/SuperStock; ©Exactostock/SuperStock; ©Mark Scott/Getty Images; ©Fancy Collection/SuperStock; ©Andreas Pollok/Getty Images; ©Ron Chapple/Getty Images; ©rSnapshotPhotos/Shutterstock; ©Peter Cade/Getty Images 28 ©Don Nichols/Getty Images 29 *(top to bottom)* ©Larry Dale Gordon/Getty Image; ©Punchstock 32 *(television)* ©Maxx-Studio/Shutterstock 35 *(top to bottom)* ©Darren Mower/Getty Images; ©Thinkstock 36 *(top row, left to right)* ©JOSE LUIS SALMERON Notimex/Newscom; ©The Everett Collection; ©The Everett Collection; ©Getty Images *(bottom row, left to right)* ©Lions Gate/courtesy Everett Collection; ©Eric Roberts/Corbis; ©Robert Voets/CBS via Getty Images; ©Ann Johansson/Corbis 40 ©violetblue/Shutterstock 43 *(left to right)* ©Maxx-Studio/Shutterstock; ©MariusdeGraf/Shutterstock 44 *(clockwise from top left)* ©Cambridge University Press; ©Artur Synenko/Shutterstock; ©Cambridge University Press; ©Cambridge University Press; ©Cambridge University Press; ©Cambridge University Press 45 ©Punchstock 47 ©Anders Blomqvist/Getty Images 48 *(left to right)* ©Ambient Images Inc./Alamy; ©Yellow Dog Productions/Getty Images; ©Spencer Grant/PhotoEdit; ©David Grossman/Imageworks 50 *(clockwise from top left)* ©Holly Harris/Getty Images; © Kwame Zikomo/SuperStock; © Jens Lucking/Getty Image; © Kaz Chiba/Getty Images; © Onoky/SuperStock; © I. Hatz/Masterfile 52 *(top row, all photos)* ©Cambridge University Press *(middle row, left to right)* ©Cambridge University Press; ©Rudy Umans/Shutterstock; ©JupiterImages *(bottom row, left to right)* ©JupiterImages; ©Cambridge University Press; ©Danilo Calilung/Corbis 56 ©Mike Powell/Getty Images 58 *(sweater)* ©Karina Bakalyan/Shutterstock; *(skirt)* ©Ruslan Kudrin/Shutterstock; *(jeans)* ©Karkas/Shutterstock *(all others)* ©Cambridge University Press 60 ©George Kerrigan 64 *(clockwise from top left)* ©Belinda Images/SuperStock; ©Ingram Publishing/SuperStock; ©Blend Images/SuperStock; ©Punchstock *(mouse)* ©urfin/Shutterstock 66 *(top row, left to right)* ©Catherine Karnow/Corbis; ©Shawn Baldwin/EPA/Newscom; ©Fotosonline/Alamy *(middle row, left to right)* ©Peter Willi/SuperStock; ©Douglas Pulsipher/Alamy; ©KSTFoto/Alamy *(bottom row, left to right)* ©Cambridge University Press; ©Prisma Bildagentur AG/Alamy; ©S.T. Yiap Still Life/Alamy 67 *(top to bottom)* ©Bob Krist/Corbis; ©Ron Erwin/Getty Images; ©Bert Hoferichter/Alamy 68 *(clockwise from top left)* ©Enzo/agefotostock; ©Olga Lyubkina/Shutterstock; ©Olga Miltsova/Shutterstock; ©Joseph Dilag/Shutterstock 69 ©Steve Hix/Somos Images/Corbis 71 *(top to bottom)* ©Laura Coles/Getty Images; ©Datacraft Co Ltd/Getty Images; ©panda3800/Shutterstock 72 *(top to bottom)* ©Stephen Johnson/Getty Images; ©Simon DesRochers/Masterfile; ©ImagesEurope/Alamy; ©David Robinson/Snap2000 Images/Alamy 75 © Best View Stock/Alamy 76 ©Thinkstock 82 ©Thinkstock 84 *(top to bottom)* ©Exactostock/SuperStock; ©Joe McBride/Getty Images 85 ©David Young-Wolff/PhotoEdit 87 ©Blend Images/SuperStock 90 *(clockwise from top left)* ©Cambridge University Press; ©Alexander Raths/Shutterstock; ©Cambridge University Press; ©Africa Studio/Shutterstock; ©Cambridge University Press; ©Cambridge University Press; ©Cambridge University Press; ©Cambridge University Press; ©Cambridge University Press; ©Lepas/Shutterstock; ©Luis Carlos Jimenez del rio/Shutterstock; ©Jonelle Weaver/Getty Images; ©Cambridge University Press; ©Tetra Images/SuperStock; ©Cambridge University Press; ©Nixx Photography/Shutterstock; ©Orange Stock Photo Production Inc./Alamy; ©simpleman/Shutterstock 91 ©jet/Shutterstock 92 *(top row, left to right)* ©Cambridge University Press; ©Cambridge University Press; ©Cambridge University Press; ©Thinkstock; ©Cambridge University Press *(top middle row, left to right)* ©Ryan McVay/Thinkstock; ©Valentyn Volkov/Shutterstock; ©Thinkstock; ©Cambridge University Press; ©Cambridge University Press *(bottom middle row, left to right)* ©Cambridge University Press; ©Cambridge University Press; ©Cambridge University Press; ©Cambridge University Press; ©Multiart/Shutterstock *(bottom row, left to right)* ©Cambridge University Press; ©Cambridge University Press; ©Cambridge University Press; ©Cambridge University Press; ©svry/Shutterstock 93 *(top to bottom)* ©Cambridge University Press; ©Thinkstock; ©Thinkstock; ©Fuse/Getty Images/RF 96 ©Lena Pantiukh/Shutterstock

Text credits

While every effort has been made, it has not always been possible to identify the sources of all the material used, or to trace all copyright holders. If any omissions are brought to our notice, we will be happy to include the appropriate acknowledgements on reprinting.

Special thanks to Kerry S. Vrabel for his editorial contributions.

The top 500 spoken words

This is a list of the top 500 words in spoken North American English. It is based on a sample of four and a half million words of conversation from the Cambridge International Corpus. The most frequent word, *I*, is at the top of the list.

1. I	40. really	79. see
2. and	41. with	80. how
3. the	42. he	81. they're
4. you	43. one	82. kind
5. uh	44. are	83. here
6. to	45. this	84. from
7. a	46. there	85. did
8. that	47. I'm	86. something
9. it	48. all	87. too
10. of	49. if	88. more
11. yeah	50. no	89. very
12. know	51. get	90. want
13. in	52. about	91. little
14. like	53. at	92. been
15. they	54. out	93. things
16. have	55. had	94. an
17. so	56. then	95. you're
18. was	57. because	96. said
19. but	58. go	97. there's
20. is	59. up	98. I've
21. it's	60. she	99. much
22. we	61. when	100. where
23. huh	62. them	101. two
24. just	63. can	102. thing
25. oh	64. would	103. her
26. do	65. as	104. didn't
27. don't	66. me	105. other
28. that's	67. mean	106. say
29. well	68. some	107. back
30. for	69. good	108. could
31. what	70. got	109. their
32. on	71. OK	110. our
33. think	72. people	111. guess
34. right	73. now	112. yes
35. not	74. going	113. way
36. um	75. were	114. has
37. or	76. lot	115. down
38. my	77. your	116. we're
39. be	78. time	117. any

The top 500 spoken words

118. he's	161. five	204. sort
119. work	162. always	205. great
120. take	163. school	206. bad
121. even	164. look	207. we've
122. those	165. still	208. another
123. over	166. around	209. car
124. probably	167. anything	210. true
125. him	168. kids	211. whole
126. who	169. first	212. whatever
127. put	170. does	213. twenty
128. years	171. need	214. after
129. sure	172. us	215. ever
130. can't	173. should	216. find
131. pretty	174. talking	217. care
132. gonna	175. last	218. better
133. stuff	176. thought	219. hard
134. come	177. doesn't	220. haven't
135. these	178. different	221. trying
136. by	179. money	222. give
137. into	180. long	223. I'd
138. went	181. used	224. problem
139. make	182. getting	225. else
140. than	183. same	226. remember
141. year	184. four	227. might
142. three	185. every	228. again
143. which	186. new	229. pay
144. home	187. everything	230. try
145. will	188. many	231. place
146. nice	189. before	232. part
147. never	190. though	233. let
148. only	191. most	234. keep
149. his	192. tell	235. children
150. doing	193. being	236. anyway
151. cause	194. bit	237. came
152. off	195. house	238. six
153. I'll	196. also	239. family
154. maybe	197. use	240. wasn't
155. real	198. through	241. talk
156. why	199. feel	242. made
157. big	200. course	243. hundred
158. actually	201. what's	244. night
159. she's	202. old	245. call
160. day	203. done	246. saying

The top 500 spoken words

247. dollars	290. started	333. believe
248. live	291. job	334. thinking
249. away	292. says	335. funny
250. either	293. play	336. state
251. read	294. usually	337. until
252. having	295. wow	338. husband
253. far	296. exactly	339. idea
254. watch	297. took	340. name
255. week	298. few	341. seven
256. mhm	299. child	342. together
257. quite	300. thirty	343. each
258. enough	301. buy	344. hear
259. next	302. person	345. help
260. couple	303. working	346. nothing
261. own	304. half	347. parents
262. wouldn't	305. looking	348. room
263. ten	306. someone	349. today
264. interesting	307. coming	350. makes
265. am	308. eight	351. stay
266. sometimes	309. love	352. mom
267. bye	310. everybody	353. sounds
268. seems	311. able	354. change
269. heard	312. we'll	355. understand
270. goes	313. life	356. such
271. called	314. may	357. gone
272. point	315. both	358. system
273. ago	316. type	359. comes
274. while	317. end	360. thank
275. fact	318. least	361. show
276. once	319. told	362. thousand
277. seen	320. saw	363. left
278. wanted	321. college	364. friends
279. isn't	322. ones	365. class
280. start	323. almost	366. already
281. high	324. since	367. eat
282. somebody	325. days	368. small
283. let's	326. couldn't	369. boy
284. times	327. gets	370. paper
285. guy	328. guys	371. world
286. area	329. god	372. best
287. fun	330. country	373. water
288. they've	331. wait	374. myself
289. you've	332. yet	375. run

The top 500 spoken words

376. they'll	418. company	460. sorry
377. won't	419. friend	461. living
378. movie	420. set	462. drive
379. cool	421. minutes	463. outside
380. news	422. morning	464. bring
381. number	423. between	465. easy
382. man	424. music	466. stop
383. basically	425. close	467. percent
384. nine	426. leave	468. hand
385. enjoy	427. wife	469. gosh
386. bought	428. knew	470. top
387. whether	429. pick	471. cut
388. especially	430. important	472. computer
389. taking	431. ask	473. tried
390. sit	432. hour	474. gotten
391. book	433. deal	475. mind
392. fifty	434. mine	476. business
393. months	435. reason	477. anybody
394. women	436. credit	478. takes
395. month	437. dog	479. aren't
396. found	438. group	480. question
397. side	439. turn	481. rather
398. food	440. making	482. twelve
399. looks	441. American	483. phone
400. summer	442. weeks	484. program
401. hmm	443. certain	485. without
402. fine	444. less	486. moved
403. hey	445. must	487. gave
404. student	446. dad	488. yep
405. agree	447. during	489. case
406. mother	448. lived	490. looked
407. problems	449. forty	491. certainly
408. city	450. air	492. talked
409. second	451. government	493. beautiful
410. definitely	452. eighty	494. card
411. spend	453. wonderful	495. walk
412. happened	454. seem	496. married
413. hours	455. wrong	497. anymore
414. war	456. young	498. you'll
415. matter	457. places	499. middle
416. supposed	458. girl	500. tax
417. worked	459. happen	

Interaction	Skills				Self study
Conversation strategies	Listening	Reading	Writing	Free talk	Vocabulary notebook
• Respond to suggestions • Use *I guess* when you're not sure	**It's good to travel.** • Predict what people are going to say about traveling, then listen for the exact words **Recommendations** • Match advice about staying at hotels with pictures, then listen to a radio show to check your answers	**Unique hotel experiences** • Read an article about three unusual hotels	**Recommendations** • Write an email about staying at one of the hotels in the lesson • Format and expressions for writing an email	**Travel smart!** • Role play: Choose a role and give your partner travel advice according to the pictures	**Travel items** • When you write down a new noun, write notes about it
• Ask politely for permission to do things with *Do you mind . . . ?* • Ask someone politely to do something with *Would you mind . . . ?* • Agree to requests	**Could you do me a favor?** • Listen to conversations between roommates, complete their requests, and then check if each person agrees **Evening routines** • Listen to someone describe his evening routine, and number pictures in order	**Do you have an unusual home habit?** • Read online comments about people's unusual home habits	**Evening routines** • Write a short article about the evening routines of your partner • Order events using sequence words	**All about home** • Pair work: Discuss questions about your homes, and find out ways you are alike and different	**The ABCs of home** • Write down a word for something in your home for each letter of the alphabet
• React to and comment on a story • Respond with *I bet . . .*	**A funny story** • Listen to an anecdote, and choose the best response **Happy endings?** • Listen to two anecdotes, and answer questions about the details	**Every cloud has a silver lining . . .** • Read a magazine article featuring anecdotes from readers	**Anecdotes** • Write an anecdote telling about a time something went wrong • Link ideas with *when* and *while*	**What was happening?** • Pair work: Look at a picture, and see how much detail you can remember about what was happening	**From head to toe** • Draw and label pictures to remember new vocabulary

Checkpoint Units 7–9   pages 95–96

Conversation strategies	Listening	Reading	Writing	Free talk	Vocabulary notebook
• Interrupt and restart phone conversations • Use *just* to soften things you say	**Sorry about that!** • Listen to three phone conversations to infer the reason for each call and for each interruption **It can be annoying . . .** • Listen to a teenager talk about texting; check the opinions she agrees with	**Why all the interest in texting?** • Read an online article about texting	**The pros and cons** • Write a short article about the advantages and disadvantages of a means of communication • Structure of an article comparing pros and cons	**Which is better?** • Pair work: Compare pairs of actions, and discuss which is better and why	**Phone talk** • Learn new expressions by making note of the situations when you can use them
• Show you're trying to remember a word or name • Use *You mean . . .* or *Do you mean . . .?* to help someone remember something	**Celebrities** • Listen to descriptions of celebrities, and match them with their photos **What's in style?** • Listen to four people answer questions about current styles, and fill in a chart	**Fashion statements** • Read a blog article about fashion trends	**Fashion trends** • Write a fashion article describing the current "look" • Expressions to describe new and old trends	**What's different?** • Pair work: Ask and answer questions to determine what's different about people in two pictures, and guess where they went	**What do they look like?** • Use new vocabulary in true sentences about yourself or people you know
• Make offers and promises with *I'll* and *I won't* • Agree to something with *All right* and *OK*	**I'll do it!** • Listen to two people planning a party, and identify what each of them says they'll do **A good idea?** • Listen to two people discussing predictions; identify who says each is a good idea and why	**What will life be like in the future?** • Read an online article with predictions about the future	**A good idea?** • Write a short article about how a future invention will make our lives better or worse • List ideas with *First*, *Second*, *Next*, and *Finally*	**I might do that.** • Pair work: Interview a classmate to find out his or her future plans	**Writers, actors, and artists** • Write new vocabulary in groups by endings or topics

Checkpoint Units 10–12   pages 127–128

Useful language for . . .

Getting help

How do you say "_____" in English?

I'm sorry. What did you say?

How do you say this word?

What do we have to do?

I don't understand. What do you mean?

Do you mean _____?

Can you spell "_____" for me, please?

Working with a partner

Whose turn is it now?

It's my / your turn.

Do you want to go first?

OK. I'll go first. / No, you go first.

This time we change roles.

OK. I'll start.

Are we done?

Yes, I think so. Let's try it again.

Let's compare answers.

OK. What do you have for number 1?

Do you have _____ for number 3?

No, I have _____ . Let's check again.

Do you understand this sentence?

Yeah. It means "_____."

Going away

 Can Do! In this unit, you learn how to . . .

Lesson A
- Talk about getting ready for a trip using infinitives to give reasons
- Give opinions using *It's* + adjective + *to*

Lesson B
- Talk about things to take on a trip
- Give advice and suggestions with *should, could, need to,* etc.

Lesson C
- Respond to suggestions
- Use *I guess* when you're not sure

Lesson D
- Read an article about unique hotels
- Write an email about a trip

1

2

3

4

Before you begin . . .
Brainstorm! Think of three . . .
- fun places to go on a trip.
- things you always take on a trip.
- fun things to do on a trip.
- different ways to travel.

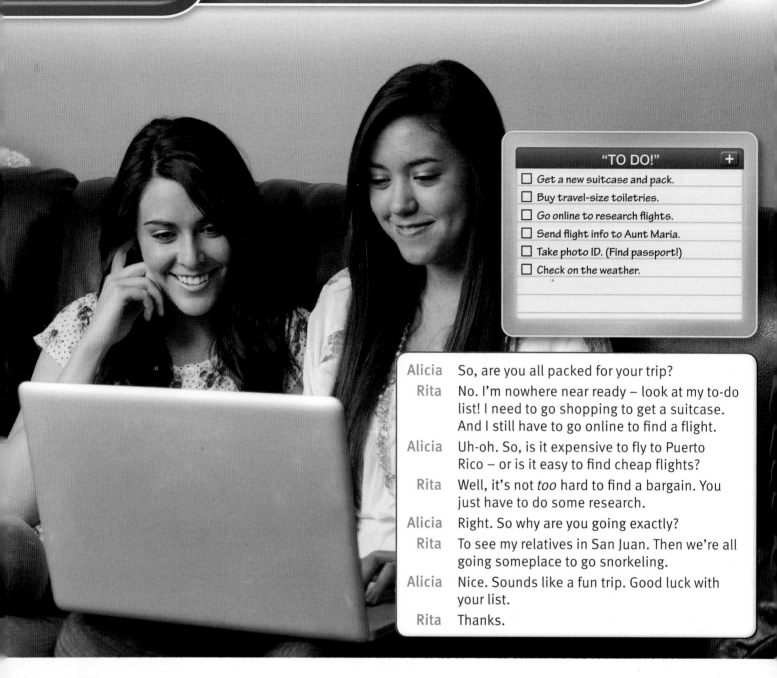

"TO DO!" +
- ☐ Get a new suitcase and pack.
- ☐ Buy travel-size toiletries.
- ☐ Go online to research flights.
- ☐ Send flight info to Aunt Maria.
- ☐ Take photo ID. (Find passport!)
- ☐ Check on the weather.

Alicia So, are you all packed for your trip?

Rita No. I'm nowhere near ready – look at my to-do list! I need to go shopping to get a suitcase. And I still have to go online to find a flight.

Alicia Uh-oh. So, is it expensive to fly to Puerto Rico – or is it easy to find cheap flights?

Rita Well, it's not *too* hard to find a bargain. You just have to do some research.

Alicia Right. So why are you going exactly?

Rita To see my relatives in San Juan. Then we're all going someplace to go snorkeling.

Alicia Nice. Sounds like a fun trip. Good luck with your list.

Rita Thanks.

1 Getting started

A Look at Rita's "to-do" list for her upcoming trip. What other things do you need to do before a trip? Make a class list.

B ◄))) 3.01 Listen. What's Rita going to do in Puerto Rico? Is she ready for the trip? Practice the conversation.

Figure it out **C** Circle the correct verb forms to complete the sentences. Use the conversation above to help you.

1. I'm going to Puerto Rico **see** / **to see** my relatives.
2. I still have to go online **to buy** / **buying** a ticket.
3. **Is it** / **Is** cheap to fly to Puerto Rico?
4. **Is** / **It's** easy to find a bargain.

2 Grammar   Infinitives for reasons; *It's* + adjective + *to* . . . 🔊 3.02

Extra practice p. 146

You can use an infinitive to give a reason.	You can use *It's* + adjective + *to* to describe a verb.
Why are you going to Puerto Rico?	**Is it** expensive **to fly**? (NOT ~~Is expensive to fly?~~)
To see my relatives.	**It's** easy **to find** a cheap flight online. (NOT ~~Is easy . . .~~)
I'm going to Puerto Rico **to see** my relatives.	**Is it** easy **to find** bargains online?
I need to go shopping **to get** a suitcase.	**It's** easy **to do**.
I have to go online **to find** a flight.	**It's** not hard **to do**.

In conversation

The top five adjectives in the structure *It's* _____ *to* . . . are *hard, nice, easy, good,* and *important.*

A Complete the conversation extracts. Use infinitives for reasons and *it's* / *is it* + adjective + *to*. Then practice with a partner.

1. A I'm going to _go to Tokyo to study Japanese_ (go to Tokyo / study Japanese) next month. I'm staying with a family on an exchange program. I just got my visa.

    B Wow! So, _____ (necessary / learn some Japanese) before you go?

    A Well, yeah. _____ (nice / say "Thank you") and things. _____ (important / know a few expressions) I think, so I want to _____ (get a phrase book / read) on the plane.

2. A I need to _____ (buy a guidebook / get some ideas) for sightseeing, too.

    B So, _____ (easy / get around) Tokyo?

    A Well, they say _____ (not hard / use the subway). But I heard _____ (easy / get lost) when you're walking around.

3. A I need to _____ (go to the bank / change some money), too. I heard _____ (good / have some cash). You know, you need to _____ (carry some cash / pay for taxis) and things.

    B _____ (not possible / pay) for everything with a credit card?

    A Not really. _____ (not easy / do) that.

B **Pair work** Choose a country to visit. Role-play a conversation about preparing for the trip. Use the conversation above for ideas. Think of more questions to ask.

A I'd love to go to Brazil to see the Carnival in Rio.

B Is it expensive to fly there?

3 Speaking naturally   Reduction of *to*

*A Is it expensive **to** visit your country?*   *B Well, it's hard **to** find cheap hotels.*

A 🔊 3.03 Listen and repeat. Notice the reduction of *to* in the sentences above.

About you **B** 🔊 3.04 Listen and complete the questions. Then ask and answer the questions with a partner.

1. Do you need a visa _____ your country?

2. Do you need to speak the language _____ your city?

3. Is it easy _____ a cheap place to stay?

4. Is it safe _____ late at night?

5. Do you have to pay _____ in museums?

1 Building vocabulary

A 🔊 3.05 Listen and say the words. What else do you see in the picture? Make a list.
Can you think of any other things you need when you travel? Compare with a partner.

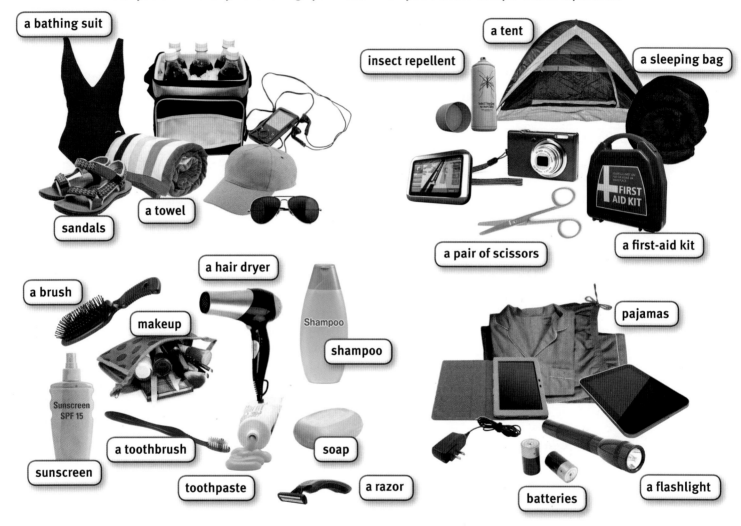

a bathing suit

a tent

insect repellent

a sleeping bag

a towel

sandals

a pair of scissors

a first-aid kit

a hair dryer

a brush

makeup

pajamas

shampoo

sunscreen

a toothbrush

soap

toothpaste

a razor

batteries

a flashlight

Word sort **B** Complete the chart using at least 15 different words. Then compare with a partner.

	You need to take . . .	It's good to have . . .	It's not necessary to take . . .
On a beach vacation	a bathing suit	sunscreen	a tent
On a camping trip			
To stay overnight with a friend			

"On a beach vacation, you need to take a bathing suit to go swimming."

Vocabulary notebook p. 74

2 Building language

A 🔊 **3.06** Listen. Jenny's going on a camping trip.
What's her mother's advice? Practice the conversation.

Mom   Jenny, maybe you should take some insect repellent. . . . Oh, and take a flashlight, and don't forget to pack some spare batteries. . . . Why don't you take my jacket? It's a good idea to have something warm. . . . Now, you need to take a hat. You could borrow your dad's. But don't lose it. . . . Oh, and Jenny, do you want to pack some other shoes?

Jenny   I'm sorry, Mom. Did you say something? I can't hear you with my headphones on.

Figure it out | **B** How does Jenny's mother make suggestions? What does she say about packing these things?

| insect repellent | a flashlight | spare batteries | her jacket | something warm | a hat | other shoes |

"You should take some insect repellent."

3 Grammar Advice and suggestions 🔊 3.07

Extra practice p. 146

What **should** I take?
Should I take these shoes?
You **should** take a hat.
You **shouldn't** take high heels.
You **could** borrow your dad's hat.
You **need to** have warm clothes.

Do you want to pack some other shoes?
Why don't you take a hat?
It's a good idea to pack a jacket.
Take a flashlight.
Don't forget to pack some batteries.

> 💬 **In conversation**
>
> *You should* . . . can be very strong. People sometimes soften it by saying:
> *I think you should* . . .
> *Maybe you should (just)* . . .
> *You should probably* . . .

A Complete the suggestions to someone going on these trips.
Then compare with a partner. Add more suggestions.

1. **a hiking trip in the Andes**
   "I think you should ___take a first-aid kit___ ."
   "It's a good idea _____ ."
   "Maybe you shouldn't _____ ."

2. **sightseeing in Paris**
   "Don't forget _____ ."
   "Why don't you _____ ?"
   "Maybe you should _____ ."

3. **a language course in Canada**
   "You need _____ ."
   "It's not a good idea _____ ."
   "You could _____ ."

4. **backpacking around Asia**
   "Take _____ ."
   "You should probably _____ ."
   "You want to _____ ."

About you | **B** **Pair work** Now look at these trip ideas. Make four suggestions to someone going on these trips.

Why don't you take some souvenirs to your relatives in the U.S.?

- visiting relatives in the U.S.
- a homestay in Japan
- a working vacation in Australia
- a road trip through California

> ❌ **Common errors**
>
> Do not use *can* to give advice.
> *I think you **should** take a first-aid kit.*
> (NOT *I think you ~~can~~ take a first-aid kit.*)

🔊 **Sounds right** p. 138

1 Conversation strategy Responding to suggestions

A Would you like to take a few days off and go away?
What would you do? Tell the class.

B ◀)) **3.08** Listen. What would Chris and Stan like to do?
What are they probably going to do?

Chris	You know, we should take a few days off sometime.
Stan	Yeah, we should. Definitely.
Chris	We could go to Mexico or something.
Stan	That's a great idea.
Chris	We could even go for a couple of weeks.
Stan	Well, maybe. I guess we could, but . . .
Chris	You know, we could just quit our jobs and maybe go backpacking for a few months. . . .
Stan	Well, I don't know. I'd like to, but . . . I guess I need to keep this job, you know, to pay for school and stuff.
Chris	Yeah, me too, I guess.

C Notice how Stan responds to Chris's suggestions with expressions like these. Find examples in the conversation.

For suggestions you like:	For suggestions you don't like:
That's a great idea.	*Maybe.*
That sounds great.	*I guess we could, but . . .*
I'd love to.	*I don't know.*
	I'd like to, but . . .

D Complete each response with an appropriate expression. Use six different expressions.
Then practice with a partner.

1. A Why don't we take a beach vacation soon?
    B _____ We can go windsurfing!

2. A You should ski with me this weekend.
    B _____ I have to work.

3. A Why don't we go to Boston next month?
    B _____ I don't have any money.

4. A Let's go camping this weekend.
    B _____ I think it's going to rain.

5. A We could go to Moscow in February.
    B _____ It's really cold in February.

6. A Let's go to New Zealand for a vacation.
    B _____ New Zealand is beautiful!

About you **E Pair work** Practice again. Use your own responses and continue each conversation.
Can you agree on something you'd both like to do?

2 Strategy plus *I guess*

You can use *I guess* when you're not 100% sure about something or if you don't want to sound 100% sure.

> I guess I need to keep this job.

> Yeah, me too, I guess.

In conversation

I guess is one of the top 20 expressions.

🔊 **3.09** Check (✓) where you think the speakers say *I guess*. Then listen and write *I guess* where you hear it. Practice with a partner.

1. A   I really prefer warm weather to cold. How about you _____ ?

   B   ✓ *I guess* I like cold weather more. It's a lot of fun to do winter sports _____ .

   A   That's true _____ . You can go sledding and stuff. We should _____ do that sometime!

2. A   So, what's your idea of a good vacation?

   B   Well, I kind of like to go camping. _____ that's my favorite thing to do.

   A   Really _____ ? That sounds like fun. Hey, why don't we go together sometime _____ ?

   B   Yeah. _____ we could go next summer, maybe.

3 Listening and strategies   It's good to travel.

A 🔊 **3.10 Pair work** Guess the missing words. Then listen to conversations between Mark and his friends. Write the missing words.

1. You have to _____ a country to really understand its culture.

2. It's important to _____ when you travel.

3. It's good to _____ tourist areas when you go somewhere.

4. It's not possible to _____ in a short trip.

5. You should try _____ when you go to a new place.

B 🔊 **3.10** Listen again. Circle the correct words to complete Mark's suggestions (A) below. Complete his friends' responses (B) with two words.

1. A   Let's go to **Mexico / Miami** this summer.

   B   I'd like to, but is it easy to find _____ _____ ?

2. A   Why don't we go to a **French / Italian** class?

   B   I guess we could, but I really want to _____ _____ .

3. A   We could **drive / hike** along the coast sometime.

   B   That sounds great. Are there any _____ _____ to stay?

4. A   We should go **scuba diving / backpacking** in Australia.

   B   I don't know. It's not easy to go. I have _____ _____ .

5. A   Do you want to go to a Chinese **exhibition / festival**?

   B   I'd love to! Do they have _____ and _____ and everything?

About you **C Class activity** Make the suggestions above to six classmates. How many say yes?

1 Reading

A Brainstorm! Do you ever stay in hotels? What's fun about staying in a hotel? Make a class list.

You don't have to cook or make your bed.
You can sit by the pool to relax.

B Read the article as quickly as you can. How much can you remember about each hotel? Compare with a partner.

> **Reading tip**
>
> If you don't understand some words in a description, find other words that will help you get a sense of their meaning. For example, *comfortable* helps you know that *cozy* means "nice in some way."

Unique Hotel Experiences

Here are three exciting hotels that you will never forget!

1. Controversy Tram Hotel, The Netherlands It's easy to see why this bed and breakfast is on our list of unusual places to stay. Don't worry – these old city trams are not going to take you anywhere. The owners got old trams from Germany and Holland and converted them into comfortable, cozy rooms with American, Italian, French, and Mexican themes. The owners sleep in an old double-decker bus from England and cook in a French van! It's definitely a place for people who like trains, planes, cars, and other transportation memorabilia.

2. EcoCamp, Chile It's not hard to fall asleep at this environmentally friendly hotel in the heart of the Torres del Paine National Park. The scenery is amazing, as is the peace and quiet. Guests stay in comfortable and inviting domes similar to the homes of ancient native peoples. You should definitely take your hiking boots. In the daytime, guests can trek through the mountains and see *guanacos* (a type of llama) and other wildlife and then go back to the domes to relax and enjoy a delicious dinner in the evening.

3. Giraffe Manor, Nairobi When we asked the owners of this African hotel, "What should we pack?" they said, "Don't forget to bring a camera." It's good to know. From the elegant rooms of this beautiful manor you have superb views of the Ngong Hills. Not only that, but a herd of giraffes lives on the manor, and you don't have to try hard to get a great photo. The giraffes wander around and poke their heads through the bedroom windows. They even turn up at the breakfast table, too.

C **Pair work** Read the article again. Discuss the questions about each hotel.

1. What is unusual about each hotel?
2. How does the article describe the rooms?
3. What can you do during the day in each place?
4. Which hotel would you like to stay at? Why?

2 Listening and writing Recommendations

A Look at these hotels. Would you like to visit any of them?

The Cave Hotel

The Lighthouse Hotel

The Spa Hotel

B ◀)) 3.11 Read the advice about staying at these hotels. Can you match each piece of advice with a hotel? Then listen and check your guesses.

1. You should bring lots of books and board games for rainy days. _2_

2. Wear flat shoes so you can climb the ladder to your room. _____

3. Be sure to take everything you need. It's miles from another town. _____

4. I really recommend the hot-air balloon ride. _____

5. Don't spend too much time in the water. _____

6. It's a good idea to have some binoculars to watch the dolphins. _____

About you **C** Imagine you are staying at one of the hotels in this lesson. Write an email to a classmate about the hotel and your trip. Use the Help note and the example below to help you.

> 🖊 **Help note**
>
> **Writing a message about a trip**
> Start like this: ▶
> Say if you are enjoying your stay: ▶
> Describe the place, food, or weather: ▶
> Say something you did: ▶
> Attach a photo and describe it: ▶
> Say something you are going to do: ▶
> End like this: ▶

New Message

Date: Aug 15

From: Sophia Davis sdavis@cup.org

Dear David,
I'm writing to you from . . .
I'm having a wonderful time here . . .
The weather is terrible, but . . .
I went out on a fishing boat yesterday and . . .
I'm attaching a photo of me on the boat . . .
Tomorrow I'm going to go hiking. . . .
See you soon! Love, Sophia.

D **Pair work** Exchange messages. Write a response to your partner's message. Make comments and ask questions for more information.

Free talk p. 132

Learning tip *Writing notes about nouns*

When you write down a new noun, it's a good idea to write notes about it.

its pronunciation and stress ▶	*phrase book (ph = /f/)*
if it's a countable or an uncountable noun ▶	*sunscreen (uncountable)*
	a map (countable)
the spelling of the singular and plural forms ▶	*a hairbrush, hairbrushes*
if it's always plural ▶	*sunglasses (always plural)*
how to make a plural noun singular ▶	*a pair of sunglasses (singular)*

1 **Match the travel items to the notes. Mark the stress on each word by underlining the stressed syllable.**

1. bathing suit ___*d*___
2. batteries _____
3. clothes _____
4. schedule _____
5. scissors _____

a. (*sc* = /s/), plural, *a pair of* (singular)
b. (sounds almost like *close*), always plural
c. (*sch* = /sk/), countable
d. (*ui* in *suit* sounds like *oo* in *too*), countable
e. ies = y (*singular*)

> **In conversation**
>
> **A pair of shoes**
>
> The top items people talk about with ***a pair of*** are:
>
> 1. shoes   5. glasses
> 2. pants   6. stockings
> 3. shorts   7. socks
> 4. jeans   8. gloves

2 **Write notes about these travel items. Add two more ideas of your own.**

pajamas   razor   shampoo   toothbrush

 On your own

Visit some travel websites and find two different types of vacations. List ten items you need for each one.

 Can Do! Now I can . . .

☑ I can . . .   ? I need to review how to . . .

- ☐ give reasons for things I do.
- ☐ give opinions with *It's* + adjective + *to*.
- ☐ discuss what I need to take on a trip.
- ☐ give advice and make suggestions.
- ☐ respond to suggestions people make.

- ☐ use *I guess* to show I'm not sure about something.
- ☐ understand conversations about travel.
- ☐ understand advice people give about hotels.
- ☐ read an article about unique hotels.
- ☐ write an email about a trip.

At home

Lesson A
- Talk about where you keep things at home
- Say who owns things with *mine*, *yours*, etc. and *whose*

Lesson B
- Talk about items in the home
- Identify things using adjectives and *one* and *ones*

Lesson C
- Use *Do you mind . . . ?* and *Would you mind . . . ?* to make polite requests
- Agree to requests with expressions like *Go right ahead* and *No problem*

Lesson D
- Read comments on a website about unusual habits
- Write about your evening routine with expressions like *first* and *as soon as*

1
on the desk
on a shelf
in a box
2
in the closet

on top of the dresser
4

3
in a drawer
under the bed
on the floor

Before you begin . . .
Look at the pictures. What do you keep in these places?

Are you a pack rat – do you hate to throw things away?

75

> **John** There's so much stuff in here! Are all these things really ours? I mean, whose bathing suit is this? Is it yours or your grandmother's?
>
> **Sandra** Hey, it's mine, and I like it.
>
> **John** And whose clothes are these?
>
> **Sandra** Oh, they're my sister's. She's storing some things here while she's away. The jewelry's hers, too. Ugh, look at these awful earrings. She has such weird taste.
>
> **John** But those are yours. I bought them for you!
>
> **Sandra** Oh, you did? Sorry. I guess they're not so bad.

1 Getting started

A Look at the picture. What are John and Sandra doing? What's in their closet?

B 🔊 3.12 Listen. Who do the clothes belong to? the jewelry? Then practice the conversation.

Figure it out **C** Circle the correct words. Use the conversation above to help you. Then compare with a partner.

1. A **Whose / Who's** bathing suit is this?
   B It's **my / mine**.

2. A **Who's / Whose** earrings are these? Are they **your / yours**?
   B No, they're my sister's. All the jewelry is **her / hers**.

3. A Does all this stuff belong to us?
   B Yes, it's all **our / ours**. They're all **our / ours** things.

2 Grammar *Whose . . . ?*; possessive pronouns ◀)) 3.13

Extra practice p. 147

Whose bathing suit is this?	It's **mine**.	It's my bathing suit.
It's **mine**. (It's my bathing suit.)	They're **yours**.	They're your earrings.
Whose jewelry is this?	It's **hers**.	It's her jewelry.
It's **hers**. (It's her jewelry.)	They're **his**.	They're his shoes.
Whose clothes are these?	They're **ours**.	They're our things.
They're **ours**. (They're our clothes.)	It's **theirs**.	It's their stuff.

In conversation

20% of the uses of *mine* are in the expression *friend(s) of mine*.

About you Complete the conversations with *whose* and possessive pronouns. Practice with a partner. Then practice again, giving your own answers.

1. A I'm always losing my keys. Do you ever lose ___yours___ ?

   B No. We always keep _____ on a shelf next to the door.

2. A Do you hang your clothes in the closet every night?

   B Well, my sister always hangs _____ in the closet, but I just throw _____ on a chair! My room's always a mess.

3. A Where do you keep your shoes? Do you have one place?

   B No, they're all over the apartment. I have three brothers, and mom's always saying, " _____ shoes are these?"

4. A What do you do with your old clothes?

   B Sometimes I give things to a friend of _____ . But my parents give _____ to charity.

5. A Where do you put your cell phone at night?

   B I always leave _____ in the kitchen. But my husband puts _____ on the dresser. It's so annoying when it rings at night. So, what do you do with _____ ?

6. A What do you do with all of your photos?

   B I put family photos on my computer. But the kids keep _____ on their phones. My husband has _____ on his tablet.

3 Speaking naturally Grammatical words

> A *Where **do you** keep **your** books?*
> B ***On a** shelf **next to my** speakers. Where **do you** keep yours?*
> A ***In a** pile **on the** floor **by my** bed.*

A ◀)) 3.14 Listen and repeat the conversation above. Notice how grammatical words like *do, you, your, on, a, next to, my, in,* and *by* are reduced. Only the content words are stressed.

About you **B Pair work** Make conversations like the one above. Use the ideas below or add your own.

- jewelry • headphones • passport • credit cards • sports equipment • music files

1 Building vocabulary

A ((•)) 3.15 Listen and say the words. What else do you see in each picture? Make a list.

Living room
- lamp
- end table
- cushions
- sofa
- armchair
- coffee table
- rug

Kitchen
- microwave
- cabinets
- faucet
- stove
- oven
- dishwasher

Bedroom
- curtains
- clock
- dresser
- nightstand
- carpet

Bathroom
- mirror
- shower
- sink
- toilet
- bathtub

Word sort **B** Complete the chart with things in your home. Then compare with a partner.

Living room	Kitchen	My room	Other
sofa	microwave		

A *In our living room, there's a sofa and . . .*

B *We don't have a sofa. We have a couple of armchairs and . . .*

 **Vocabulary notebook** p. 84

2 Building language

A 🔊 3.16 Listen to these people shopping online. Which items does Meg like? Which items does Jon like? Do they have the same tastes?

1

Jon	I need a new cover for my tablet. Which one do you like?
Meg	That nice black leather one there.
Jon	Hmm, I prefer the blue one in the middle.
Meg	Which one? The blue one with the orange dots? Really?
Jon	Yeah. It's really cool.

2

Jon	Oh, and I need some new speakers, too. Which ones do you like? The rectangular black ones?
Meg	Um, those cute little round ones are cool.
Jon	How about the orange ones on the right?
Meg	Hmm. Well, they go with the tablet cover, I guess.

Figure it out

B **Pair work** Choose the correct words. Then practice with a partner.

A I like that **black nice / nice black** tablet cover.

B I like that blue **one / ones** in the middle.

A And do you like those cute **round little / little round** speakers?

B Which **one / ones**? The orange **one / ones**?

> ✕ **Common errors**
>
> Don't put an adjective after a noun.
>
> *I like the* **round** *speakers.*
> (NOT *I like the* ~~speakers round~~*.*)

3 Grammar Order of adjectives; pronouns *one* and *ones* 🔊 3.17

Extra practice p. 147

Usual adjective order
opinion, size, shape, color, nationality, material
They have a **beautiful black leather** cover.
I want those **cute little round** speakers.

I like the black cover. Which **one** do you like?
 I like the blue **one** in the middle.
Those speakers are cool. Which **ones** do you like?
 I like the silver **ones** on the left/right.

> 💬 **In conversation**
>
> People usually use just one or two adjectives before a noun.

About you Complete the sentences so they are true for you. Then practice with a partner.

1

metal   plastic   wooden

I don't like the _____ .
Which _____ do you prefer?

2

small   medium   large

I like the _____ .
Which _____ do you like?

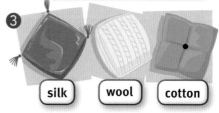

3

silk   wool   cotton

I'd like to have the _____ .
Which _____ would you like?

A I like the big metal mirror. Which one do you like?

B Well, I like the small pink one in the middle. The one with the plastic frame.

🔊 **Sounds right** p. 138

1 Conversation strategy Asking politely

A How can you make visitors to your home feel welcome when they arrive? What do you do or say?

B 🔊 3.18 Listen. What does Lucy ask permission to do? What request does Adam make?

Adam	Hi Lucy! Come on in.
Lucy	Thanks. I brought you some flowers. Are the others here yet?
Adam	No, not yet. So just make yourself at home. Thanks for these. Can I take your coat?
Lucy	Sure. Thanks. This is a great apartment. Do you mind if I look around?
Adam	No, go ahead.
Lucy	Oh, I love this antique table. It's beautiful.
Adam	Yeah, it's great, but it's not really mine. It's my mother's.
Lucy	Well, she has great taste.
Adam	Yeah. Listen, I hate to ask this, but I'm running a bit late. Would you mind helping me in the kitchen?
Lucy	No, not at all. What can I do?
Adam	Well, . . . could you chop the onions?
Lucy	No problem. I'm happy to help.

C Notice how Lucy uses *Do you mind if. . . ?* to ask for permission, and Adam uses *Would you mind . . . -ing?* to ask Lucy to do something. Also notice that they answer "no" to show they agree. Find the examples in the conversation.

"Do you mind if . . . ?"
"No, go ahead."
"Would you mind . . . -ing?"
"No, not at all."

D Pair work Imagine you are visiting your partner's home. Take turns asking permission to do these things and agreeing to the requests. Can you think of more ideas?

1. make a quick call
2. open a window
3. use your bathroom
4. take a cookie
5. get a glass of water
6. charge my phone

"Do you mind if I make a quick call?"   *"No, go ahead."*

E Pair work Imagine your partner is visiting your home. Take turns asking him or her to do these things and agreeing to the requests. Can you think of more ideas?

1. answer the door for me
2. put this in the trash
3. set the table for me
4. make some coffee
5. help me with the dishes
6. turn on the oven

"Would you mind answering the door for me?"   *"No, not at all."*

2 Strategy plus Agreeing to requests

Answer Yes to agree to requests with Can and Could:

Can I look around?
  Yes. / Sure. / Go (right) ahead.
Could you chop the onions?
  Yes. / Sure. / OK. / No problem.

Answer No to agree to requests with mind:

Do you mind if I look around?
  No, go (right) ahead. / No, not at all.
Would you mind helping me in the kitchen?
  No, not at all. / Oh, no. No problem.

> **In conversation**
> *Do you mind ___ing . . . ?* and *Would you mind if I . . . ?* are possible but not very common.

◀)) 3.19 **Listen and complete the answers. Then practice with a partner.**

1. A Do you mind if I sit here?

   B _____ . Let me move my things.

2. A Could you do me a favor? Could you run to the store and get some milk?

   B _____ . What kind of milk do you want?

3. A I forgot to charge my phone. Can I borrow yours for a minute?

   B _____ . It's on the coffee table there.

4. A I think I left my wallet at home. Uh, would you mind lending me five dollars?

   B _____ . Here, I have ten dollars.

3 Listening and strategies Could you do me a favor?

A ◀)) 3.20 **Listen to four conversations between roommates. What's the problem in each case?**

1. _____   3. _____
2. _____   4. _____

B ◀)) 3.21 **Can you guess what favors each person is going to ask? Listen and complete the sentences. Do their roommates agree? Check (✓) the boxes.**

		Agrees	Doesn't agree
1. Can you _____ ?		☐	☐
2. Would you mind _____ ?		☐	☐
3. Could you do me a favor? Could you _____ ?		☐	☐
4. Do you mind if I borrow _____ ?		☐	☐

C Class activity Ask your classmates for favors.

You want someone to . . .

- help install software on your laptop.
- find a phone number online for you.
- introduce you to their friend.

You need . . .

- to borrow some headphones.
- some money to buy some gum.
- help with some homework.

    A *Hey, Jen, would you mind helping me install some software on my computer?*
    B *Oh, I'm sorry. I'm not very good at computer stuff. I can't even do that on mine!*

1 Reading

A Circle the words to make these statements true for you. Tell the class.

- My kitchen is very **organized** / **disorganized**.
- I wash dishes **by hand** / **in the dishwasher**.
- I iron **none** / **some** / **all** of my clothes.
- I **save** / **throw out** used food containers.

B Read the comments on the website. What habits do the people have? Which do you think are unusual?

> **Reading tip**
> Ask yourself questions as you read, for example, *Is this logical? Is this normal?* etc.

http://www.personalhomestyle... +

Do you have an unusual HOME HABIT?

view all | favorites

Post comment

Martin_442   March 31, 10:55 p.m.   [read full comment] [reply]

Well, my best friend has a very disorganized kitchen, but you should see mine. As soon as I come back from grocery shopping, I organize everything. First, I arrange the cans so the vegetables are in one section and the canned fruit is in another section. Next, I sort them by size so the big ones are at the back and the small ones are at the front. Then I make sure I can see all the labels.

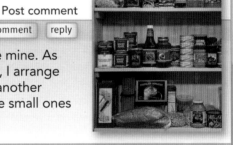

Charlotte   April 21, 8:02 p.m.   [read full comment] [reply]

We have a brand new expensive dishwasher, but I hate it. I don't think it washes very well. My friend says hers is great, but mine always leaves the glasses dirty. So I always wash the dishes by hand before I load them in the dishwasher. Then, after I take them out, I rinse them again to make sure they are clean! It drives my husband crazy!

Lucia_P   April 22, 7:55 a.m.   [read full comment] [reply]

My weird home habit? I iron everything, including my jeans, while I'm watching TV. I even iron my socks. My roommate just stuffs hers in a drawer, but I like to fold everything, too. I even iron the curtains in my bedroom every two weeks. I know it sounds crazy, but you iron yours, too, right?

Manas_No_more_chores   April 22, 7:58 a.m.   [read full comment] [reply]

OK, I can't help it. I save every small plastic take-out container, pizza box, cups from the coffee shop, salad cartons, etc. My friend just throws all his in the trash, but I think that's a waste. You can use them for a lot of different things. Like the big cardboard pizza boxes – we use ours during the summer for picnic trays.

C Read the comments again. Answer the questions.

1. How does Martin arrange the cans in his cupboards?
2. Why does Charlotte wash the dishes before she puts them in the dishwasher?
3. What does Lucia iron?
4. What does Manas do with the containers he saves?

About you **D** **Pair work** What unusual habits does your family have? Tell your partner.

2 Listening Evening routines

About you   **A** Do you do any of these things when you get home every day? Tell the class.

B 🔊 **3.22** Listen. What does Mike do when he gets home? Number the pictures in the correct order.

C 🔊 **3.22** Listen again and answer the questions. Is your evening like Mike's?

1. What does Mike take out of his pockets at night? Why?

2. When does he do the dishes? Why?

3. How does he feel after he exercises? After he watches the news?

4. What does he do just before he goes to sleep?

3 Speaking and writing Evening routines

About you   **A** Write answers to the questions below. Then ask and answer the questions with a partner. How are your routines the same?

- What do you do as soon as you get home?
- What do you do before you have dinner?
- What do you do while you're eating?
- What's your bedtime routine?

About you   **B** Read the article below. Then write an article about your evening routine. Use the expressions in the Help note that order events.

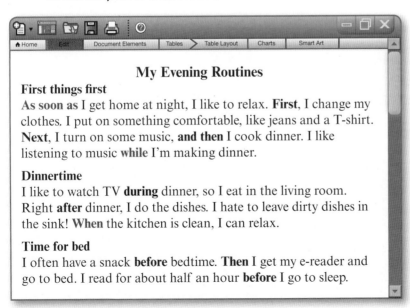

My Evening Routines

First things first
As soon as I get home at night, I like to relax. **First**, I change my clothes. I put on something comfortable, like jeans and a T-shirt. **Next**, I turn on some music, **and then** I cook dinner. I like listening to music **while** I'm making dinner.

Dinnertime
I like to watch TV **during** dinner, so I eat in the living room. Right **after** dinner, I do the dishes. I hate to leave dirty dishes in the sink! **When** the kitchen is clean, I can relax.

Time for bed
I often have a snack **before** bedtime. **Then** I get my e-reader and go to bed. I read for about half an hour **before** I go to sleep.

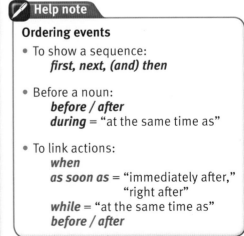

Help note

Ordering events

- To show a sequence:
  first, next, (and) then

- Before a noun:
  before / after
  during = "at the same time as"

- To link actions:
  when
  as soon as = "immediately after," "right after"
  while = "at the same time as"
  before / after

Free talk p. 133

Learning tip *Alphabet game*

Make learning new words into a game! Choose a topic and try to think of a word for each letter of the alphabet.

1 Label the pictures. The first letter of each word is given for you.

a _____   b _____   c _____   d _____

2 Now complete your own alphabet chart. Can you think of something in your home for each letter?

a armchair	h	o	v
b	i	p	w
c	j	q	x
d	k	r	y
e	l	s	z
f	m	t	
g	n	u	

On your own

Make labels for different things in your home. Don't throw the label away until you can remember the new word.

Can Do! Now I can . . .

✓ I can . . .   ? I need to review how to . . .

- ☐ talk about where I keep things at home.
- ☐ say who owns things.
- ☐ talk about furniture and home furnishings.
- ☐ identify and describe which things I mean.
- ☐ ask politely for permission to do things.
- ☐ ask other people to do things.

- ☐ agree to requests.
- ☐ understand requests for favors and replies.
- ☐ understand details about evening routines.
- ☐ read comments about unusual home habits.
- ☐ write about my evening routine.

Things happen

 Can Do! In this unit, you learn how to . . .

Lesson A
- Tell anecdotes about things that went wrong using the past continuous and simple past

Lesson B
- Talk about accidents (e.g., *I broke my arm.*) using the past continuous and *myself, yourself,* etc.

Lesson C
- React to show interest with expressions like *Oh, no!*
- Use *I bet* to show you're sure or that you understand

Lesson D
- Read anecdotes in an article
- Write an anecdote using *when* and *while*

1

2

3

4

Before you begin . . .

Look at the pictures. Think about a time when one of these things happened to you. Tell the class about a time when you . . .

- broke something.
- lost something.
- forgot something.
- damaged something.

85

Are you having a BAD week?

Sean Davis

Actually, yes. I was going to work on the train Monday morning, and I was talking to this woman. I guess I wasn't paying attention, and I missed my stop. I was half an hour late for a meeting with my new boss.

Julia Chen

Definitely! My friend accidentally deleted all my music files when she was using my computer. Actually, she was trying to help me – she was downloading stuff from my phone, and something went wrong. I spent hours on the phone with tech support.

Roberto Moreno

Yeah, kind of. A couple of days ago, a friend and I were trying to look cool in front of some girls at the mall. We weren't looking, and we walked right into a glass door. I was so embarrassed.

1 Getting started

A Look at the illustrations above. What do you think happened to each person? Do these kinds of things ever happen to you? Tell the class.

B ◀)) **3.23** Listen and read. Were your guesses about the people correct?

Figure it out **C** Can you choose the correct verb forms? Use the interviews above to help you. Then compare with a partner.

1. Sean **missed** / **was missing** his stop because he **talked** / **was talking** to a woman on the train.

2. Julia's friend **deleted** / **was deleting** all Julia's music files when she **using** / **was using** her computer.

3. Roberto and his friend **tried** / **were trying** to look cool when they **walked** / **were walking** into a glass door.

2 Grammar Past continuous statements ◀)) 3.24

Extra practice p. 148

Use the past continuous to set the background for a story or tell about events in progress in the past. Use the simple past for completed actions in the past.
I **was talking** to a woman, and I missed my stop. I **wasn't paying** attention.
We **were trying** to look cool, and we walked into a glass door. We **weren't looking**.
A friend of mine deleted all my music files **when** she **was using** my computer.
When my friend **was using** my computer, she deleted all my music files.

In conversation

The most common verbs in the past continuous are *talk, do, go, say, try, get,* and *tell.*

**Complete the anecdotes with the past continuous or simple past.
Then close your book. Take turns retelling the anecdotes to a partner.**

1. I ___was having___ (have) lunch in a café yesterday when the server accidentally _____ (spill) tomato sauce on my shirt. I guess he _____ (not / pay) attention. I was upset, but I _____ (get) my lunch for free.

2. My friend and I were at a barbecue last week. When we _____ (walk) around the yard, she _____ (trip) and _____ (fall) into the pond.

3. I _____ (damage) my parents' car last week. I _____ (try) to park, and my friend _____ (talk) to me, and I _____ (hit) a wall. Now I have to pay for the repairs.

4. I was in a chemistry class recently, and a classmate and I _____ (do) an experiment when something _____ (go) wrong. I _____ (burn) my hand.

5. Last week I was on the bus, and I _____ (talk) to my girlfriend on my cell phone. Well, actually, we _____ (have) a long argument. We _____ (not / get along) at the time. When I _____ (end) the call, I realized that everyone on the bus _____ (listen). How embarrassing!

3 Speaking naturally Fall-rise intonation

*I was running for a **bus** last week, and I **fell**.*
*When I was going **home** yesterday, I ran into an old **friend**.*

A ◀)) 3.25 Listen and repeat the sentences above. Notice that the intonation falls and then rises slightly at the end of the first part of each sentence. This sets the background.

B ◀)) 3.26 Listen and complete the sentences. Then listen again and repeat.

1. I was reading a book _____ , and I missed my stop.
2. Last night when I was washing _____ , I broke a glass.
3. I was texting _____ , and I tripped and fell on the street.
4. Yesterday when I was using _____ , it suddenly crashed.

About you C Pair work Think of things that happened to you this week. Tell each other your anecdotes.

1 Building vocabulary

A 🔊 3.27 Listen and say the words and sentences. Which words and expressions do you already know?

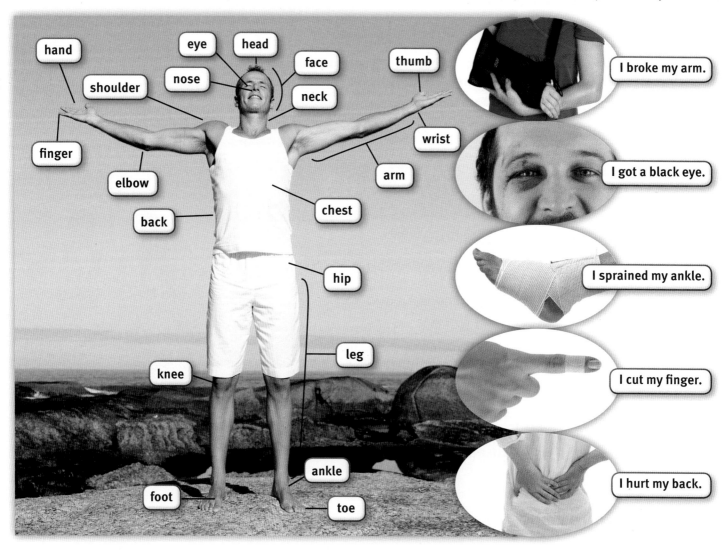

hand · eye · head · face · nose · shoulder · neck · thumb

I broke my arm.

finger · elbow · back · chest · arm · wrist

I got a black eye.

I sprained my ankle.

hip · leg · knee

I cut my finger.

foot · ankle · toe

I hurt my back.

Word sort **B** Make true sentences about accidents that happened to you or people you know. Use the vocabulary above and add other words you know.

break	I broke my leg when I was a kid.
sprain	
cut	
hurt	
other	My sister got a black eye . . .

About you **C** Pair work Take turns telling about the accidents in your chart.

Vocabulary notebook p. 94

2 Building language

A 🔊 **3.28** **Listen. What happened to George? What was he doing when it happened? Practice the conversation.**

Nikki So, how was your ski trip? Did you have a good time?

George Yeah, I guess. I sort of had an accident.

Nikki Oh, really? What happened? Did you hurt yourself?

George Yeah, I broke my leg.

Nikki Oh, no! How did it happen? I mean, what were you doing?

George Well, actually, I was talking on my cell phone. . . .

Nikki While you were skiing? That's kind of dangerous.

George Yeah, I know. But I was by myself, so I was lucky I had my cell to call for help.

Figure it out **B** **Complete the questions George's other friends asked. Use the conversation above to help you.**

1. What **were** / **did** you doing?
2. How **did it happen** / **was it happening**?
3. Did you hurt **yourself** / **you**?
4. I don't enjoy skiing **by** / **with** myself. Do you?

3 Grammar Past continuous questions; reflexive pronouns 🔊 3.29

Extra practice p. 148

Past continuous	Simple past	Reflexive pronouns	
Were you **skiing** with a friend?	**Did** you **hurt** yourself?	I	myself.
No, I wasn't. I was by myself.	Yes, I did.	You	yourself.
What **were** you **doing** (when you fell)?	What **did** you **do**?	He	himself.
I was talking on my cell phone.	I called for help.	She — hurt —	herself.
		We	ourselves.
		They	themselves.

In conversation

10% of uses of *yourself* are in the question *How about yourself?* Almost 10% of uses of *myself* are in the expression *by myself*.

✗ Common errors

Don't use an object pronoun when the subject and object of the verb refer to the same person.

*My father hurt **himself**.* (NOT ~~My father hurt him.~~)

A **Complete the conversations with reflexive pronouns and the simple past or past continuous of the verbs given.**

1. A What's wrong with your finger? Did you cut _____ ?

   B Yeah, I accidentally cut _____ with a knife.

   A Oh, _____ you _____ (make) dinner?

2. A My father hurt _____ at the gym.

   B That's too bad. _____ he _____ (lift) weights?

   A Yeah. A lot of people hurt _____ on weight machines, I guess.

3. A Hey, where _____ you _____ (get) that black eye?

   B Oh, my mom and I had a car accident. But she's OK.

   A Well, that's good. Uh, so who _____ (drive)?

4. A My sister was hiking by _____ last weekend, and she broke her ankle. She was in the middle of nowhere.

   B Oh, no! So, how _____ she _____ (get) help? I mean, _____ anyone else _____ (hike) on the trail?

🔊 Sounds right p. 139

B **Pair work** **Practice the conversations above. Continue them with your own ideas.**

1 Conversation strategy Reacting to a story

A Look at some words from a funny story. Can you guess what happened?

curry   *phone*   *burnt pan*   *hide*   *hilarious*

B 🔊 3.30 Listen. What happened to Hugo? How did he "solve" his problem?

Hugo I was at my friend's house one time. We were making Thai curry for a bunch of people . . .

Olivia Oh, I love Thai food.

Hugo And he left me in the kitchen to watch the curry. Well, my phone rang and I got talking . . .

Olivia Uh-oh.

Hugo . . . and it all stuck to the bottom of the pan and burned.

Olivia Oh, no!

Hugo Yeah. It didn't taste too good. I freaked.

Olivia I bet.

Hugo So I poured the curry into another pan and added some chili peppers. Then I hid the burnt pan under the sink.

Olivia Oh, that's hilarious. I bet no one even noticed.

Hugo I don't know. No one said anything, but they drank a lot of water.

C Notice how Olivia reacts to Hugo's story. She makes brief comments on the things he says to show she is listening and interested. Find examples in the conversation.

> *"It all stuck to the bottom of the pan and burned."*
>
> *"Oh, no!"*

D Read the story below and the comments on the right. For each part of the story, choose a comment. Practice telling the story and commenting with a partner.

1. I was working as a server at Pierre's last year. __c__
2. Yeah, it's very fancy with cool art and everything. _____
3. Well, it's not cheap. Anyway, I was serving coffee to this guy, and I spilled it all over his suit! _____
4. Yeah – but wait. I found out it was Pierre himself! _____
5. Yeah, and he was pretty mad. But he didn't fire me! _____

a. Oh, no! I bet he was upset.
b. Well, that was lucky.
c. Oh, Pierre's is nice, I heard.
d. Expensive, huh?
e. You're kidding, the owner?

2 Strategy plus *I bet* . . .

You can start a statement with *I bet* . . . when you are pretty sure about something.

> I hid the burned pan under the sink.

> I bet no one even noticed.

You can also use *I bet* as a response to show you understand a situation.

A *I freaked!*
B *I bet.*

In conversation

Bet is one of the top 600 words. Over 60% of its uses are in the expression *I bet* . . .

🔊 **3.31 Read the stories and guess the responses. Then listen and write the responses you hear. Practice with a partner.**

1. A A friend of mine was staying at a hotel one time, and she was walking back to her room in the dark, and she fell in the pool. Everyone at the pool café saw her!

    B Oh, no! I bet _____ .

2. A One time I fell asleep on the subway, and when I woke up, the train was at the end of the line. It took an hour to get back to my stop.

    B Oh, I bet _____ .

3. A I was on vacation in London with my parents a few years ago, and we were flying home. Anyway, we got to the airport, and I realized my passport was still in the hotel safe.

    B Oh, no. I bet _____ .

3 Listening and strategies A funny story

A 🔊 **3.32 Listen to the story. Choose the best response each time you hear a pause. Check (✓) a or b.**

1. a. ☐ That's awful.   b. ☐ Oh, I bet.
2. a. ☐ I bet.   b. ☐ Nice.
3. a. ☐ It's easy to do.   b. ☐ That's good.
4. a. ☐ I bet.   b. ☐ Thank goodness.
5. a. ☐ I bet he was pretty upset.   b. ☐ Good.

About you **B** 🔊 **3.32 Listen to the story again. Write your own comments or responses when you hear the pauses.**

1. _____   4. _____
2. _____   5. _____
3. _____

C Pair work Take turns retelling the story you just heard, or tell your own story. React with short comments and respond using *I bet.*

Reading

A Brainstorm! Make a list of any good things that happened recently. Tell the class.

I passed my final math test.
My friend gave me a ticket to a concert.

B Read the article. What bad thing happened to each person? Did their stories have happy endings?

> 📖 **Reading tip**
>
> As you read a story, pay attention to the time expressions like *ten years later*, or *last month*. They help you follow events.

EVERY CLOUD HAS A SILVER LINING . . .

GEMMA RUSSO, CALIFORNIA

Sometimes when things go wrong, they just go wrong. But occasionally something really positive comes out of a bad situation. Last month, while I was hiking in a state park, I took a photo of an amazing sunset over a lake. It was so beautiful that I decided to text it to my friend Charley right then and there. Anyway, when I was taking more photos of the lake, I slipped and dropped my cell phone in the water. Disaster! I lost all my photos, and I sprained my ankle. They couldn't fix my phone, either. Well, apparently, Charley secretly sent in my sunset photo to the local TV station. Today, they chose it for "Photo of the Month," and I won a brand new camera! Maybe every cloud does have a silver lining, after all!

CHIN-HO, DAEGU

A couple of weeks ago, I was helping a friend move his things into my apartment. He was out of work and needed a place to stay. While we were carrying some heavy boxes up the stairs, I hurt my back. It was really bad, so I had to go to the emergency room. Anyway, while I was waiting to see the doctor, I saw an advertisement for a computer technician at the hospital. I called my friend, he got the job, and I got a prescription for painkillers! At least his cloud had a silver lining! Though I do have my apartment all to myself again.

ELENA, TEXAS

Ten years ago, my scooter broke down when I was riding to school. I couldn't afford to fix it, so that semester I had to get up at 5:00 a.m. every day to take the bus. One cold, wet morning, I was feeling really tired and grumpy. But while I was waiting for the bus, this guy started talking to me, and he actually made me laugh! It turned out that he was studying at the same college. We exchanged phone numbers, and the rest is history. Ten years later, we're married with two children. Oh, and a new scooter!

C Read the article on page 92 again. Are the sentences true or false?
Check (✓) *True* (T) or *False* (F). Correct the false sentences.

		T	F
	occasionally		
1.	Gemma believes that something good ~~always~~ comes out of a bad situation.	☐	☑
2.	Gemma won a new camera because she sent her photo to a local TV station.	☐	☐
3.	Elena had to take the bus to class because she didn't have the money to fix her scooter.	☐	☐
4.	Elena liked the guy at the bus stop because he was funny.	☐	☐
5.	Chin-ho hurt himself when he was trying to help a friend.	☐	☐
6.	Chin-ho's friend moved to a new place when he got the job at the hospital.	☐	☐

2 Listening and speaking Happy endings?

A ◀)) 3.33 Listen to Gary's and Pam's stories. Who lost something? Who got lost?

B ◀)) 3.33 Listen to the stories again. Answer the questions.

Gary's story

1. Where was Gary? What was he doing?
2. Who did he meet?
3. Why did he forget his briefcase?
4. What did he do when he got to work?
5. Does this story have a happy ending?
   Why or why not?

Pam's story

1. Where was Pam going?
2. What was her problem?
3. How did she get help?
4. How did the woman offer to help?
5. Does this story have a happy ending?
   Why or why not?

C **Pair work** Student A: Choose one of the stories above, and retell it to a partner.
Student B: Listen. Did your partner leave out any important details?

Free talk pp. 134 and 136

3 Writing Anecdotes

A Think of a time something went wrong. Write 10 to 12 sentences about it. Make sure your
sentences are in order.

I was walking to work last week.	The light changed.
It started to rain.	I had to wait for a really long time.
I didn't have an umbrella.	A young man came up to me.
I put a newspaper over my head and ran.	He offered to share his umbrella.
I got to the corner.	He walked with me all the way to work!

About you **B** Read the Help note and the anecdote. What events do the words *when* and *while* link?
Then use your notes from above to write your own anecdote.

Last week, I was walking to work **when** it started to
rain. I didn't have an umbrella, so I put a newspaper
over my head and ran. **When** I got to the corner, the
light changed, and I had to wait for a really long
time. **While** I was waiting, a young man came up to
me and offered to share his umbrella. He walked
with me all the way to work! It was so nice of him.

Help note

Linking ideas with *when* and *while*.

You can use *when* or *while* to link a longer "background" event
and another action.
- *While* emphasizes the length of time an action or event takes.
- *When* also shows events that happen one after another.

C **Group work** Read your classmates' anecdotes. Which ones show "every cloud has a silver lining"?

Vocabulary notebook — From head to toe

Learning tip *Sketches*

Draw and label pictures to help you remember new vocabulary.

In conversation

Take my hand

The top ten body parts people talk about are:

1.	hand	6.	arm
2.	eye	7.	mouth
3.	head	8.	ear
4.	face	9.	back
5.	leg	10.	knee

1 Label the sketch. Use the words in the box.

eye
nose
head
face
neck
shoulder

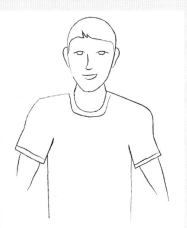

2 Now make a sketch of a body from head to toe. How many parts of the body can you label?

 On your own

Before you go to sleep each night, think of the name for each part of your body. Start at your head, and work toward your toes. Can you think of each word in English before you fall asleep?

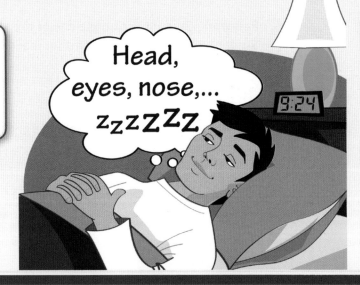

Head, eyes, nose,... zzzZZz

9:24

 Can Do! Now I can . . .

✓ I can . . .   ? I need to review how to . . .

- ☐ tell anecdotes about things that went wrong.
- ☐ talk about accidents and what happened.
- ☐ react with expressions like *Oh, no!* to show I'm listening to a story.
- ☐ use *I bet* to show I'm sure or as a response to show I understand.

- ☐ understand people telling anecdotes and respond.
- ☐ understand the details of a story.
- ☐ read anecdotes in an article.
- ☐ write an anecdote about something that went wrong.

1 Can you complete this conversation?

A Complete the conversation. Use the simple past or past continuous of the verbs.

Marty Where ___*did*___ you ___*get*___ (get) that black eye?
_____ you _____ (fall) or something?

Kevin Not exactly. I _____ (crash) into a tree with a bike.

Marty You're kidding! How _____ that _____ (happen)?

Kevin Well, I _____ (ride) my little brother's bicycle. And his friends _____ (watch) me and _____ (laugh) at me.

Marty So why _____ they _____ (laugh)? I mean, what _____ you _____ (do)?

Kevin I _____ (not do) anything special. But the bike is kind of small.

Marty Yeah, I bet. And I bet you _____ (try) to look cool, too.

Kevin I guess. I _____ (look) at the kids behind me. And I _____ (not see) the tree ahead of me. When my brother _____ (shout), "Watch out," I _____ (turn) around, but it was too late.

Marty Oh, no! _____ you _____ (hurt) yourself?

Kevin Well, I _____ (not break) anything. I just _____ (feel) embarrassed.

B Pair work Practice the conversation. Then practice again and change Marty's responses.

2 What's in the bathroom?

A Look at the picture for ten seconds, and try to remember where things are. Then close your book. How many sentences can you write?

> *1. There's a toothbrush on the sink.*

B Pair work Choose six items from the picture. Give your partner clues to guess the items. Then change roles.

A *You use it to clean your teeth.*
B *Is it a toothbrush?*
A *No, it's not.*
B *Is it toothpaste? . . .*

3 Can you use these expressions?

Use these words and expressions to complete the conversation. Use capital letters where necessary.

whose	yours	one	bright	would you mind	I guess	by myself	no, not at all
mine	hers	red	to do	✓ do you mind if	I bet	yourself	

Karen   _Do you mind if_ I come in? You look busy.

Trish   No, make _____ at home. _____ handing me that paintbrush? The red _____ ?

Karen   _____ .

Trish   Thanks. So, what do you think?

Karen   Um, nice. I love the _____ _____ wall. Did you and your roommate choose the colors together?

Trish   No, actually, I did it all _____ . Nadia's away this week.

Karen   Oh, is she? _____ this was a lot of work.

Trish   Actually, no. It was very easy _____ .

Karen   _____ room is this? Is it _____ or Nadia's?

Trish   This one is _____ , and _____ is down the hall.

Karen   Um, does Nadia like these colors?

Trish   I don't know. But I do! _____ I have an eye for color.

4 Suggestions, please!

Pair work Think of solutions to these problems. Then take turns making suggestions.

"I get a lot of colds in the winter."

"My bedroom is always a mess."

"I'm going camping in June, but I don't have any equipment."

"Ouch! I think I just sprained my ankle."

A *I get a lot of colds in the winter.*

B *Why don't you . . . ?*

5 Do you mind . . . ?

Pair work Imagine you and your partner are in a car on a road trip. One of you is the driver. Take turns asking permission and making requests. Use the ideas below and add your own.

- turn on the air conditioning
- listen to the radio
- check the GPS
- stop for a snack
- drive
- slow down
- open the window
- borrow some sunscreen
- eat one of your cookies

A *Would you mind turning on the air conditioning?*

B *No, not at all.*

Communication

10

 Can Do! In this unit, you learn how to . . .

Lesson A	Lesson B	Lesson C	Lesson D
• Compare ways of communicating using comparative adjectives	• Manage phone conversations • Compare communication habits using *more*, *less*, and *fewer*	• Interrupt and restart a phone conversation • Use *just* to soften what you say	• Read an article about texting • Write an article giving pros and cons

Before you begin . . .

Match these ways of communicating with the pictures.
Which of these do you do?

- ☐ texting
- ☐ video calling
- ☐ video conferencing
- ☐ instant messaging (IM)
- ☐ social networking

HOW DO YOU KEEP IN TOUCH WITH PEOPLE?

"We use email at work, but I use my social network to keep in touch with friends. I was getting a lot of spam in my personal email. There's nothing worse than spam in your inbox."

—Alma Jones

"Well, at work we use video conferencing for meetings with our international offices. It's less expensive than a business trip. And more convenient. And you don't get jet lag, either!"

—Kayla Johnson

"I text my friends all day. Texting's a lot quicker and easier than calling. It's more fun, too. I can't do it in class, though."

—Mayumi Sato

"Well, I video call my parents. They think it's better than the phone because they can see me. I guess it's a good way to keep in touch when I'm away at school."

—Paco Rodriguez

"Well, for birthdays and things I still like to send a card. I know regular mail is slower and less reliable than email, but cards are more personal. And I never send those e-cards. I just think it's nicer to get a real card."

—Tim Henry

1 Getting started

A 🔊 **4.01** Listen to the responses to the survey question. How do the people keep in touch?

Figure it out **B** Can you complete the sentences? Circle the correct words. Use the survey to help you.

1. Mayumi says texting is **quicker** / **quick** than calling. It's more fun **than** / **that** calling, too.
2. Tim thinks real cards are more **personal** / **nice** than e-cards.
3. Kayla says that video conferencing is **less** / **more** expensive than a business trip.
4. Paco's parents think that video calling is **good** / **better** than phone calls.
5. Alma says nothing is **worse** / **bad** than spam in your inbox.

2 Grammar Comparative adjectives ◀))) 4.02

Extra practice p. 149

Short adjectives *Adjective + -er*	Texting is **quicker** and **easier than** calling. It's **nicer** to get a real card than an e-card.
Long adjectives *more* + adjective *less* + adjective	Real cards are **more personal than** e-cards. Video conferences are **less expensive than** trips.
Irregular adjectives **good** ▶ **better** **bad** ▶ **worse**	Video calls are **better than** phone calls. Nothing is **worse than** spam in your inbox.

Notice
slow ▶ slow**er**
nice ▶ nic**er**
easy ▶ eas**ier**
big ▶ big**ger**

But
fun ▶ **more** fun

In conversation

The top adjectives after *more* are *expensive, convenient, important, interesting,* and *fun.*

A Complete the conversations with the comparative form of the adjectives and *than* if needed. Then practice with a partner.

1. A Do you like e-cards? I think they're _more interesting than_ (interesting) real cards.

   B True. And they're _____ (easy) to send, too. Though they're a bit _____ (personal) real cards.

2. A Do you ever use video calling? Our grandparents think it's _____ (nice) because they can see us. It's _____ (good) the phone.

   B Yeah, and it's _____ (expensive) international phone calls.

3. A Do you prefer your tablet or your laptop?

   B My laptop. It's _____ (big), but it's _____ (useful) a tablet. Tablets are _____ (difficult) to work on.

   A Yeah? My sister prefers her tablet. She says it's _____ (light) her laptop, so it's _____ (convenient) to carry around.

4. A Do you use email much these days? I don't. I just use my social network.

   B Me too. It's _____ (efficient) email. And it's _____ (fun). It's _____ (good) texting, too. Texting's _____ (bad) email.

About you **B** **Pair work** Ask and answer the questions above. Give your own opinions.

Common errors

With comparatives, use *more* or *-er,* not both.

IM is **easier** than email. (NOT IM is ~~more easier~~ than email.)

3 Speaking naturally Linking

*With social networking, it**'s ea**sier to kee**p i**n touch with people.*

*Text message**s a**re les**s e**xpensive than phone calls.*

*Real card**s a**re nicer tha**n e**-cards.*

A ◀))) 4.03 Listen and repeat. Notice how the consonants are linked to the vowels.

About you **B** ◀))) 4.04 Listen and repeat the questions below. Then discuss the questions in groups.

1. How do you kee**p i**n touch with friend**s a**nd family?
2. Do you talk to your grandparent**s e**very day?
3. Do you u**se a** social network to communicate with friends?
4. I**s i**t easier to text your friend**s o**r to call them?
5. Do you think video call**s a**re more fun than phone calls?

1 Building vocabulary

A 🔊 4.05 Listen and read. Why can't Nathan have a conversation with Angela?

① **Receptionist** Good afternoon. Sun Company.
Nathan Hello. **Could I speak to** Angela Bell, please?
Receptionist One moment, please.
Voice mail Angela Bell is on the phone. Please leave a message.
Nathan **Hi,** Angela. **This is** Nathan. **Call me back on my cell.**

② **Angela** Angela Bell.
Nathan Hi, Angela. It's Nathan. Did you get my message?
Angela Uh, yes, I think so. **Oh, hold on. I have another call.** Call me later, OK?

③ **Woman** Hello?
Nathan Uh, Angela?
Woman No, this is Beth.
Nathan Oh, **I'm sorry. I think I have the wrong number.**
Woman No problem.

④ **Angela** Hello?
Nathan Hi, Angela. Guess what!
Angela Nathan, I can't hear you. **You're breaking up.** Call me back on my office phone.
Nathan Oh, OK.

⑤ **Angela** Angela Bell.
Nathan Angela! Listen. My boss has some concert tickets for us. . . . Uh, Angela? Angela? Oh, no! **We got cut off.**

Word sort

B Find these expressions in the phone conversations, and write them in the chart. Then practice the conversations with a partner.

What can you say when . . .	
you ask to speak to someone?	
you leave a voice-mail message?	
you want someone to return your call?	
you need to interrupt because you have another call?	
you call someone by mistake?	
you can't hear some of the other person's words?	
the phone call suddenly ends?	

2 Building language

A 🔊 4.06 Listen to the conversation Nathan and Angela finally have. Why was Nathan calling?

Nathan Finally! It's hard to get ahold of you.

Angela You're not that easy to reach, either.

Nathan You spend a lot more time on the phone than I do.

Angela That's because I get more calls.

Nathan You just talk more! Anyway, I was calling before 'cause my boss had free tickets to the Sting concert tonight.

Angela Oh, great! What time?

Nathan Well, it's too late now. He gave them to someone else.

Angela Oh, no! Why didn't you send me a text message?

Figure it out **B** Can you rewrite these sentences and keep the same meaning? Start with the word given. Use the conversation above to help you.

1. Angela You get fewer calls than I do. I _____ .

2. Nathan I spend less time on the phone than you do. You _____ .

3. Nathan I talk less than you do. You _____ .

3 Grammar *More, less, fewer* 🔊 4.07

Extra practice p. 149

With countable nouns	With uncountable nouns	With verbs
I get **more** calls than you (do).	I spend **more** time on the phone.	She talks **more** than he does.
You get **fewer** calls than I do.	You spend **less** time on the phone.	He talks **less** than she does.

In conversation

Fewer is not very common. People use it more in writing.

About you **A** Complete the sentences with *more*, *less*, or *fewer* so they are true for you. Rewrite them in a different way and keep the same meaning.

1. My friends talk __more__ than I do.   *I talk less than my friends do.*

2. On the phone, I listen _____ than I talk.

3. I send _____ emails than texts.

4. I spend _____ time on social networking sites than my parents.

5. I get _____ emails than I did two years ago.

6. I get _____ voice-mail messages than text messages.

7. My parents talk on the phone a lot _____ than I do.

8. I like texting _____ than calling.

B Pair work Discuss the sentences above. Compare your styles of communication.

A *I think my friends talk more than I do. I'm pretty quiet.*

B *Really? I talk more than all my friends. They say I never stop talking!*

(((• Sounds right p. 139

What were you saying?

1 Conversation strategy Dealing with interruptions

A What kinds of things can interrupt phone conversations? Make a list.

B 🔊 4.08 Listen. What does Maria want to tell Sarah?

Sarah	Hello?
Maria	Hi, Sarah. It's Maria.
Sarah	Hey. How are you doing?
Maria	Great. Listen, I have some news. Juan and I went out to a fancy restaurant last night and . . .
Sarah	Oh, just a minute. I've got another call. Hold on a second. . . . Sorry. So, what were you saying?
Maria	Well, guess what? We're getting married.
Sarah	That's wonderful! Congratulations!
Maria	Thanks. So yeah, the wedding's going to be in . . .
Sarah	Oh, sorry. Now there's someone's at the door. Hold on. . . . OK. So, you were saying?
Maria	Well, I was just calling to ask – will you be my maid of honor?
Sarah	Are you kidding? Of course!

C Notice how Sarah interrupts the conversation and then comes back to it with expressions like these. Find examples in the conversation.

Interrupting a conversation:	Restarting the conversation:
Just a minute / second.	*What were you saying?*
Excuse me just a second.	*You were saying?*
I'm sorry. Hold on (a second).	*Where were we?*
Could / Can you hold on a second?	*What were we talking about?*

D 🔊 4.09 Listen. Complete these phone conversations with the expressions you hear. Then practice with a partner. Continue the conversations using your own ideas.

1. A So yeah. I just read on a friend's social networking page that . . .

   B Oh, _____ . . . . I need my charger. OK. Got it. So, _____ ?

2. A Anyway, my teacher told me . . .

   B Oh, _____ . My toast is burning. Let me just – gosh . . . OK. _____ . So, yeah. _____ ?

3. A Sorry about that. I dropped my phone. So, _____ ?

   B You said your social life is more important than your job. Oh, _____ . Um, a coffee, please. Sorry. I'm at a coffee shop. So, _____ ?

2 Strategy plus *just*

You can use the word *just* to make the things you say softer.

> Just a minute. I've got another call.

> I was just calling to ask . . .

🔊 4.10 **Listen to four phone conversations. Write *just* each time the speakers use it. Then practice the conversations with a partner.**

📋 **In conversation**

Just is one of the top 30 words.

1. A Hi there. Do you have a minute? I *just* want to tell you some good news.
   B Really? Hold on a second. I need to close the door.

2. A Hello?
   B Hi, Dad. It's me. Is Mom there?
   A Yeah. But hold on a second. She's upstairs. I need to call her.

3. A Is this a good time to talk?
   B Sure. Could you hold on a second? Let me turn down the TV. . . . So, what's up?
   A Well, I was calling to ask your advice about something.

4. A Hi, I'm calling to say hello.
   B Oh, hi. Listen, can I call you back? I have to finish something.

3 Listening and strategies Sorry about that!

A 🔊 4.11 **Listen to the conversations. Why is each person calling? Write the reasons under the pictures.**

❶

❷

❸

_____ _____ _____

B 🔊 4.11 **Listen again. Check (✓) the reasons for the two interruptions in each conversation.**

1. ☐ She got another call.
   ☐ They lost the connection.
   ☐ Her battery ran out.
   ☐ She ordered a coffee.

2. ☐ The TV wasn't working.
   ☐ There was traffic noise.
   ☐ She dropped her phone.
   ☐ The pizza arrived.

3. ☐ He had to find his wallet.
   ☐ He met a friend.
   ☐ He went the store.
   ☐ She had to turn off the oven.

About you **C** **Pair work** Student A: "Call" and tell your partner some interesting news. Student B: "Answer" your partner's call. Interrupt and restart the conversation twice. Then change roles.

A *Hey, Jake. How are you? Do you have a minute? I just want to tell you something.*

B *Hi. So, what's going on? Oh, hold on a second. I need to take this call. It's my mom.*

📓 **Vocabulary notebook** p. 106

Reading

A Is texting a good way to communicate? Why or why not? Make a list of reasons.

B Read the article. What's one advantage of texting? What's one disadvantage?

 Reading tip

Read the first and last paragraph of an article to get a general sense of what it is about.

---

 15 Comments

Why all the interest in texting?

ICYC*: Textese Today
(*In Case You're Curious)

LOL – Laugh out loud

:-) – Smile

SUP – What's up?

FBM – Fine by me

OTOH – On the other hand

IMO – In my opinion

An article on the Internet recently caught my eye. It was about the Texting Championships in New York City. The 17-year-old winner texted 149 characters in 39 seconds and won $50,000. That is certainly impressive, and much, much faster than me – LOL :-). However, I started to wonder: Why is there still so much interest in texting? After all, texting is a commonplace activity these days.

It's clear that texting, with all its abbreviations and symbols, is now part of our lives. According to research, about 75% of Americans send text messages, and almost one third prefer to text rather than talk on their phone. It's just quicker to send a text than make a call. Typing SUP is faster than asking "How are you?" and listening to the answer. It's also more discreet because no one can overhear your conversation – and that's FBM.

OTOH, texting has its downsides, too, and perhaps it's these problems that create all the interest. Texters gripe that they are getting more spam texts than ever before. Teachers complain that students' test scores are getting worse because teens spend more time texting than they should. Some also say that texting encourages bad grammar and punctuation and IMO, that's true. Students don't realize they shouldn't write their essays in "textese," and they get low grades as a result. Many young people are sleeping less because they wake up in the night every time a text pops up on their phone. Others have injuries to their hands and thumbs from the constant texting.

There are also more serious problems with texting, however, such as the accidents that happen when people text and drive at the same time. Fortunately, many countries are passing laws that make it illegal to text when you're behind the wheel of a car. In addition, public service advertisements warn of the dangers of texting while driving. Perhaps, then, there is good reason for all the interest in texting.

C Read the article again and answer the questions. Then compare with a partner.

1. Why do so many people like texting better than talking on the phone? Find two reasons.
2. How many texting abbreviations does the author of the article use? What does each one mean?
3. What is "textese"? What kinds of problems does it cause?
4. What are some other downsides of texting? Find four problems in the article.
5. Do you have any advice for people who text all the time? Write four "Dos" and "Don'ts" for texters.

D   Find the expressions below in the article on page 104. What do they mean?
Match each one to a definition. Write *a* to *f*.

1. caught my eye _____
2. wonder _____
3. discreet _____
4. overhear _____
5. downsides _____
6. warn of _____

a. disadvantages
b. not noticeable
c. hear without intending to
d. got my attention
e. say there's a problem
f. ask myself

2   Speaking and listening   It can be annoying . . .

About you   **A**   **Pair work**   Read the sentences below. Which ones do you agree with? What else can you
say about texting?

☐ Texting takes less time than calling.
☐ Texting your parents in public is less embarrassing than talking on the phone.
☐ Texting is useful when you ask a favor.

☐ It's annoying to get texts late at night.
☐ When you're with a friend, it's OK to text other friends.
☐ You shouldn't text friends during class.

B 🔊 **4.12**   Listen to Vanessa talk about texting. Check (✓) the sentences she agrees with.

3   Writing   The pros and cons

A   **Pair work**   Choose one of these ways of communicating. Make a list of its advantages
and disadvantages.

• video calling   • texting   • social networking   • phone calls   • email

Advantages of video calling
• It's fun to video call with a close friend.
• It's either very cheap or free.
• It's almost like you're in the same room.

Disadvantages of video calling
• People call me when I don't look very good. It's embarrassing!
• People talk longer on a video call. It's harder to say good-bye.

B   The article below is divided into four sections. What is the purpose of each section? Read the Help
note for an explanation. Then use your list from above to write a similar article.

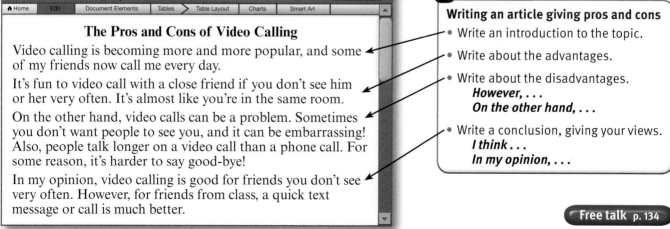

The Pros and Cons of Video Calling

Video calling is becoming more and more popular, and some of my friends now call me every day.

It's fun to video call with a close friend if you don't see him or her very often. It's almost like you're in the same room.

On the other hand, video calls can be a problem. Sometimes you don't want people to see you, and it can be embarrassing! Also, people talk longer on a video call than a phone call. For some reason, it's harder to say good-bye!

In my opinion, video calling is good for friends you don't see very often. However, for friends from class, a quick text message or call is much better.

🖊 **Help note**

Writing an article giving pros and cons
• Write an introduction to the topic.
• Write about the advantages.
• Write about the disadvantages.
  However, . . .
  On the other hand, . . .
• Write a conclusion, giving your views.
  I think . . .
  In my opinion, . . .

Free talk   p. 134

About you   **C**   **Group work**   Read your classmates' articles. Whose opinions do you agree with?

Learning tip *Learning expressions*

One way to learn expressions is to make a note of the situations when you can use them.

In conversation

Hold on!

People mostly say **Hold on** to leave a phone conversation for a minute.

▮▮▮▮	*Hold on.*
▮▮▮	*Hang on.*
▮▮	*Just a minute.*

1 Match the expressions with the situations.

1. "I'm sorry. I have the wrong number."_____
2. "I have another call." _____
3. "You're breaking up."_____
4. "We got cut off." _____
5. "Where were we?" _____

a. You can't hear someone clearly.
b. You call the wrong number by mistake.
c. You come back to a conversation after an interruption.
d. You get a signal that a second person is calling you.
e. You suddenly can't hear the other person at all.

2 Make a chart of expressions you can use on the phone when . . .

- you have problems getting ahold of someone
- you have problems with the call while you're talking.
- you ask if it's a good time to talk.
- you need to interrupt the conversation.

- you ask to speak to someone.
- you explain why you're calling.
- you restart the conversation.
- you can't talk now, but you can talk later.

 On your own

Make a phrase book for different situations – for example, making calls. Carry it with you, and learn the phrases.

Can I call you back?

My Phrase Book

Can Do! Now I can . . .

✓ I can. . .   ? I need to review how to . . .

- ☐ talk about different ways of communicating.
- ☐ make comparisons.
- ☐ manage phone conversations.
- ☐ interrupt and restart phone conversations.
- ☐ use *just* to soften what I say.

- ☐ understand basic phone conversations.
- ☐ understand someone giving opinions about texting.
- ☐ read an article about the pros and cons of texting.
- ☐ write an article giving pros and cons.

Appearances

Lesson A
- Describe people's appearance using adjectives and *have* and *have got*

Lesson B
- Identify people by their appearance, actions, or location using verb + *-ing* and prepositions

Lesson C
- Use expressions like *What do you call . . . ?* if you can't remember a word
- Use expressions like *You mean . . . ?* to check or suggest words and names

Lesson D
- Read an article about fashion
- Write an article about fashion trends

Jennifer   Andrea   Erica   Donald   Sarina   Nancy   John   Maddie

Before you begin . . .

Look at the picture. Can you find someone who . . .

- is short?
- is tall?
- is young?
- is old?
- is thin?
- is heavy?
- has long hair?
- has short hair?
- has dark hair?
- has blond hair?

Alice	What does your twin sister look like, Heather? Do you look alike? I mean, are you identical twins?
Heather	No, we look totally different. Hayley's a lot taller than me. She takes after my dad.
Alice	How tall is she?
Heather	Six three.*
Alice	Huh? . . . *How* tall is she?

Heather	Six foot three. I'm serious.
Alice	No kidding! So, does she have curly black hair like you?
Heather	No, she's got straight blond hair and blue eyes. And she's thinner than me, too. I mean, she's really skinny.
Alice	She sounds like a model.
Heather	Actually, she is a model!

*six (foot) three = one meter ninety

1 Getting started

A Describe the people in the picture above. Can you find someone with curly hair? With straight hair? Someone who is tall and skinny?

B 🔊 4.13 Listen. Alice and Heather are meeting Heather's twin sister, Hayley, at the airport. Can you find Hayley in the picture? Practice the conversation.

Figure
it out **C** Use the conversation above to help you complete these questions and answers. Then practice with a partner.

1. A _____ does your sister look like?

   B She's tall, and she's _____ blond hair.

2. A _____ tall is your sister?

   B Six foot three. We're different. We don't look _____ .

108

2 Grammar Describing people; *have got* ◄)) 4.14

Extra practice p. 150

Do Hayley and Heather **look alike**?
No, they look totally different.

What does Hayley **look like**?
She's tall and thin.

Who does she **look like**?
She looks like her father.

Saying heights
Her father is six (foot) seven. He's six foot seven inches (tall).
She's one meter ninety (tall).

How tall is her father?
He's six (foot) seven.
He's over two meters tall.

What color is Hayley's hair?
It's blond.

What color are Hayley's eyes?
They're blue.

have got = have
Does she **have** curly hair?
No, she**'s got** straight hair.
Who**'s got** curly hair?
I do. I**'ve got** curly hair.

Who's got = Who has got
I've got = I have got
He's got = He has got

> **✗ Common errors**
>
> Don't confuse these questions:
> *What's she like?*
> = What kind of person is she?
>
> *What does she look like?*
> = Can you describe her?

> **✗ Common errors**
>
> Don't forget to use a form of *have*.
>
> *She's got long brown hair.*
> (NOT ~~She got~~ long brown hair.)

A Choose the correct words to complete the questions.
Compare with a partner.

1. (How)/ **What** tall are you?
2. What color **have** / **are** your eyes?
3. **Who** / **What** do you look like – your mother or your father?
4. **What** / **How** color is your mother's hair? **Is it** / **Are they** long or short?
5. **What** / **How** does your father look like?
6. Does anyone in your family **have** / **got** blue eyes?
7. Who **'s got** / **got** short hair in your class? Does anyone **got** / **have** long hair?
8. Do any of your friends look **alike** / **like** someone famous?
9. Do you know any twins? Do they look exactly **like** / **alike**?

About you **B** **Pair work** Ask and answer the questions above. Give your own information.

3 Speaking naturally Checking information

Asking for information	A *What's his **name**?*	A *How **old** is he?*	A *What color is his **hair**?*
	B *Joshua Murray.*	B *Ninety-five.*	B *White.*
Checking information	A ***What's** his name?*	A ***How** old is he?*	A ***What** color is his hair?*

A ◄)) 4.15 Listen and repeat the questions and answers above. Notice how the stress and intonation are different in the checking questions.

About you **B** **Pair work** Ask your partner to describe a good friend. Ask information questions and checking questions to make sure your information is correct.

A *So, tell me about your friend. What's her name?*
B *Her name's Kat.*
A *What's her name?*
B *Kat. It's short for Katrina.*

1 Building vocabulary

A 🔊 **4.16** Listen and say the sentences. Check (✓) the features you like. Tell the class.

"I like mustaches."   *"I like muscular people."*

①
☐ He has **a beard** and **a mustache**.

②
☐ She has **pierced ears**.

③
☐ He has **a shaved head**. He's **bald**.

④
☐ She wears **braces**.

⑤
☐ She has **long fingernails**.

⑥
☐ He wears his hair in **a ponytail**.

⑦
☐ She's got **freckles**.

⑧
☐ She wears her hair in **cornrows**.

⑨
☐ She wears **glasses**.

⑩
☐ He's very **muscular**.

⑪
☐ She wears **braids**.

⑫
☐ He's got **spiked hair**.

Word sort **B** For each feature, think of someone you know, and write a sentence. Then compare with a partner.

1. My boss has a beard and a mustache.
2. My mother's got pierced ears.

📔 **Vocabulary notebook** p. 116

2 Building language

A 🔊 **4.17** Listen. Find Rosa's roommate and Rosa's brother in the picture. Practice the conversation.

Jason	So, is your new roommate here?
Rosa	Ava? Yeah, she's right over there.
Jason	Oh, which one is she?
Rosa	She's the woman standing by the table.
Jason	The one with the short hair?
Rosa	No, the woman with the ponytail.
Jason	Oh, she looks nice. And who's that guy talking to her? He looks kind of weird.
Rosa	You mean the guy in the yellow pants? That's my brother Jimmy.

Figure it out **B** Can you complete these sentences about Ava and Jimmy? Use the conversation above to help you.

1. Ava is the woman _____ by the table.
   She's the one _____ the ponytail.

2. Jimmy is the guy _____ to Ava.
   He's the one _____ the yellow pants.

3 Grammar Phrases with verb + *-ing* and prepositions 🔊 **4.18**

Extra practice p. 150

Which one is your roommate?	Who's the guy **talking** to Rosa's roommate?
She's the woman ⎡ **standing** by the table. ⎣ **wearing** (the) black pants.	The guy **wearing** (the) yellow pants? My brother. The guy **standing** by the table is my brother.
She's the one ⎡ **by** the table. ⎢ **with** (the) long hair. ⎣ **in** the black shirt.	Who's the guy **in** the blue shirt? Which one? The one **with** (the) glasses? That's Jason. The guy **with / in** (the) yellow pants is Rosa's brother.

A Choose the correct words in the questions. Then look at the picture above, and match the questions and answers. Ask and answer the questions with a partner.

1. Who's the tall man **in** / (**in the**) striped shirt? __c__
2. Who's the woman **talks** / **talking** to Jimmy? _____
3. Who's the guy **with** / **in** the shaved head? _____
4. Who's the woman **stand** / **standing** by Alex? _____
5. Who's the woman **in** / **with** the black curly hair? _____
6. Is Jason the one **is eating** / **eating** a cookie? _____

a. Yes. He's the one talking to Rosa.
b. In the white skirt and red top? That's Olivia.
c. In the yellow pants? That's Jimmy.
d. The muscular one? That's Alex.
e. The short blond one? That's Ava.
f. The one in the green blouse? That's Rosa.

About you **B** Pair work Ask and answer questions about people in your class.

A *Who's the guy sitting next to Claudia?*
B *The one in the blue shirt? That's Marco.*

🔊 **Sounds right p. 139**

1 Conversation strategy Trying to remember words

A Do you know what these things are? Match the words and the descriptions.

1. a goatee _____
2. a wig _____
3. cargo pants _____
4. platform shoes _____

a. shoes with thick soles
b. baggy pants with pockets
c. a little short beard
d. false hair

B 🔊 4.19 Listen. What does Gabby tell Jin-ho about their old classmate?

Gabby Do you remember that cool guy in our class last year? Oh, what's his name? You know . . . he always wore those baggy pants with all the pockets. What do you call them?

Jin-ho You mean cargo pants.

Gabby Yeah. And he had long hair and a funny little beard . . . what do you call that?

Jin-ho Do you mean a goatee? . . . Oh, I know. You mean Max!

Gabby That's right, Max. Well, don't look now, but he's sitting right behind you. And he's wearing a suit and tie and everything.

Jin-ho A suit and tie? No way!

Gabby Yeah, and he's got short hair. He looks different!

C Notice how Gabby uses expressions like these when she can't remember a name or a word. Find examples in the conversation.

What's his / her name?
What do you call it / them?
What do you call that . . . / those . . . ?

D Complete the conversations with expressions like the ones above. Then practice with a partner.

1. A Do you remember when everyone wore those shoes – _____ – the ones with really thick soles?

   B Oh, yeah. Platform shoes. Actually, people still wear them!

2. A A friend of mine wears her hair in those tiny braids – _____ ?

   B Cornrows? They're really cool.

3. A Who's that singer with all the amazing clothes? _____ ? You know, her hair always looks different because she wears those, uh – _____ ?

   B Do you mean wigs? Are you thinking of Lady Gaga?

2 Strategy plus *You mean . . .*

You can say *You mean . . .* or ask *Do you mean . . . ?* to check what someone is talking about or to suggest a word or name.

> Do you mean a goatee? . . . Oh, I know. You mean Max.

What words are these people trying to think of? Write a response using *You mean . . .* or *Do you mean . . . ?* Then practice with a partner.

1. A I'm going to buy a pair of those baggy pants with lots of pockets. What do you call them?
   B *You mean cargo pants.*

2. A My brother has long hair, and he pulls it back, you know, he wears it in a, um . . .
   B _____

3. A My best friends are twins. They look exactly alike. They're, uh, what do you call them?
   B _____

4. A My friend has these cute little spots on her nose. What do you call them?
   B _____

5. A My grandfather doesn't have any hair. He's, uh, what do you call that?
   B _____

6. A When I was a kid, I wore those, what do you call those things on your teeth. Um, . . .
   B _____

3 Listening and strategies Celebrities

A 🔊 **4.20** Listen. Two friends are watching an awards ceremony on TV, and they are talking about the celebrities. Who are they talking about? Number the pictures 1 to 6.

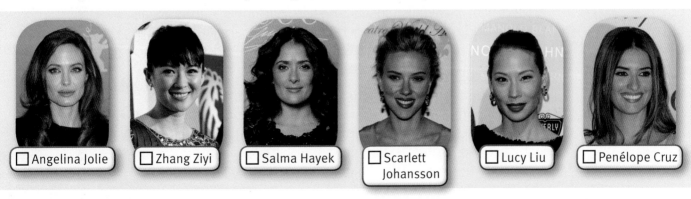

☐ Angelina Jolie ☐ Zhang Ziyi ☐ Salma Hayek ☐ Scarlett Johansson ☐ Lucy Liu ☐ Penélope Cruz

B Pair work Take turns talking about celebrities as if you can't remember their names. Can your partner guess who you are talking about?

A I really like that singer from Colombia. What's her name? She sings in English, Spanish, and Arabic.

B Oh, do you mean Shakira? Yeah, her voice is amazing.

> **Free talk** pp. 135 and 136

1 Reading

A What clothes and hairstyles are in fashion right now? When did they become fashionable?

B Read the blog. Which styles do you know about? Which do you like?

> **Reading tip**
>
> Practice skimming. Read the first sentence of each paragraph to get a general idea of what the article is about.

http://www.fashionstatement...

BLOG   FASHION TRENDS   PICTURES   RUNWAY SHOWS   SALES   CONTRIBUTE

FASHION STATEMENTS

A few days ago, I pointed out my twelve-year-old niece to a friend. "She's the one wearing braces – the *pink* ones." I realized at that moment that *braces* are now a fashion statement. Can you imagine? But then, did you ever imagine that plastic shoes with holes in them would become so popular all those years ago? Or that you could buy little charms to wear on them?

But that's the great thing about fashion. You're never quite sure what's going to become the "in" thing.

Take glasses. Big glasses came and went, and then everyone wanted designer glasses with a logo. Men wore glasses with heavy, black frames for a time. Then colored frames were the "in" thing, and soon people didn't want frames at all. Glasses, too, became a fashion statement, and people wore them even if they didn't *need* glasses!

Hairstyles are another great way to make a fashion statement. Men with ponytails, shaved heads, cornrows – they've all come and gone and come back into style again. Women's hairstyles are long and straight one minute, and short and curly the next. Bangs are in. Oh wait, no . . . bangs are out.

Then of course, there are jeans. Straight-legged are the way to go, until everyone wears them flared. Some guys wear them baggy. *Really* baggy. Women, on the other hand, seem to prefer "skinny jeans." Black jeans are in, and then everyone starts wearing white jeans, or pink jeans, or . . . every other color.

One thing is for sure. It's a lot of work keeping up with the latest fashion trends – and *expensive*! Maybe the best way to make a fashion statement is to do your own thing and not follow fashions at all!

C Read the blog again. Answer the questions.

1. Why does the writer say that braces are now a "fashion statement"?
2. What shoe style became popular years ago?
3. What five styles of glasses does the writer mention? Do you know anyone who wears any of them?
4. How many hairstyles for men does the writer list? Do you have any friends with these styles?
5. What is the opposite of baggy jeans? straight-legged jeans? Which style do you prefer?
6. What advice does the writer give about keeping up with the latest fashion trends? Do you agree?

2 Listening What's in style?

A 🔊 4.21 Listen to a fashion editor interview four people. What items are they talking about? Write the number of the conversations (1 to 4) next to the items. There is one extra item.

shirts _____   shoes _____   skirts _____   dresses _____   pants _____

B 🔊 4.21 Listen again. What specific fashion is each person talking about? How does the person feel about that style? Complete the chart. Do you agree with each person?

	Fashion	Does she / he like it? Why or why not?
1. Leslie		
2. Emery		
3. Kara		
4. Franz		

3 Speaking and writing Fashion trends

About you **A** Group work Ask and answer the questions. Take notes on the different ideas.

1. What clothes are "in" today among your friends?
2. What clothes are going out of style?
3. What styles of shoes are your friends wearing?
4. What do you like about today's "look"?
5. What don't you like about it?

B Read the article below and the Help note. Underline the expressions in the article that describe trends.

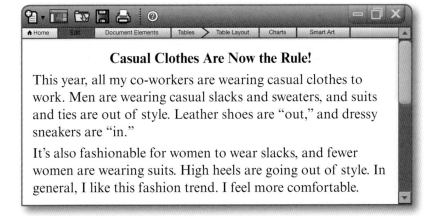

Casual Clothes Are Now the Rule!

This year, all my co-workers are wearing casual clothes to work. Men are wearing casual slacks and sweaters, and suits and ties are out of style. Leather shoes are "out," and dressy sneakers are "in."

It's also fashionable for women to wear slacks, and fewer women are wearing suits. High heels are going out of style. In general, I like this fashion trend. I feel more comfortable.

✎ **Help note**

Describing new trends

*Short hair is **in style**.*
*Long hair is going **out of style**.*
*High heels are **dated / old-fashioned**.*
*Glasses are becoming **popular**.*
***It's fashionable** to wear . . .*

Less formal expressions
*Short hair is **"in"** or **"out."***
*Glasses are the **"in" thing**.*
*They're very **trendy**.*

C Write an article describing the current "look." Use at least four of the expressions in the Help note.

Learning tip *Writing true sentences*

Use your new vocabulary in true sentences about yourself or people you know.

1 **What do these people look like? Match the sentences and people.**

1. He's tall, and he's got spiked hair. ___d___
2. She has short hair. _____
3. He's bald, and he wears glasses. ——
4. She's wearing earrings. ——
5. She wears her hair in braids. ——

6. He's short and a little heavy. _____
7. She's got freckles. _____
8. She has long hair and big brown eyes. _____
9. He's got blue eyes and blond hair. _____
10. She has dark curly hair. _____

2 **Write three sentences about each of these people. What do they look like?**

- a family member
- a classmate
- a close friend
- yourself
- another person

On your own

Look at three different people this week.
Think of how to describe them.
Then write sentences.

He's green and bald and...

NOW PLAYING

MY FRIEND THE ALIEN

Can Do! Now I can . . .

✓ I can . . .   ? I need to review how to . . .

- [ ] describe people's appearance and features.
- [ ] identify people by saying what they are doing, how they look, or where they are.
- [ ] use expressions like *What do you call . . . ?* when I'm trying to remember a word.

- [ ] use *(Do) you mean. . . ?* to check or suggest a word.
- [ ] understand which person someone is describing.
- [ ] understand people's opinions about fashion.
- [ ] read an article about fashion trends.
- [ ] write an article about fashion trends.

Looking ahead

 Can Do! In this unit, you learn how to . . .

Lesson A
- Make predictions and discuss future plans with *will*, *may*, and *might*

Lesson B
- Talk about jobs
- Discuss future plans using the simple present in *if* and time clauses

Lesson C
- Make offers and promises with *will*
- Agree to something using *All right* and *OK*

Lesson D
- Read an article about the future
- Write an article about an invention using *first*, *second*, etc. to list ideas

Before you begin . . .

Which of these things do you think you are going to do in the next five years? How sure are you? Absolutely sure? Pretty sure? Not at all sure?

- get an interesting job
- find your own place
- move to a new city
- travel to another country

WHAT ARE YOUR PLANS FOR NEXT YEAR?

1 "Well, I'm graduating from college next June, so I guess I'll look for a job. I know it won't be easy to find one – so I may go on for a master's degree. We'll see."

–Christy Lewis

2 "I'm not sure. I might look for a better job. Before that, though, I'm going to ask my boss for a promotion. But I probably won't get one, so . . ."

–Laura Chang

3 "Well, some of my friends are going to travel around Europe for two months. I hope I'll be able to go with them. But it'll be expensive, and I might not be able to afford it."

–Paul Reade

4 "We're going to have a baby in March, so both of us will probably take some time off from work. I'm sure the baby will keep us both very busy."

–Jim and Katie Conley

5 "I'm going to retire – I'll be 65 in June – and my wife's already retired. So we'll probably move to Florida in the fall, or maybe Arizona. We're not going to spend another winter here – that's for sure!"

–Joe Etta

1 Getting started

A 🔊 **4.22** Are you going to do any of these things next year? Tell the class. Then listen. What are the people above going to do? Check (✓) the boxes below.

☐ have a baby   ☐ graduate from college   ☐ buy a house   ☐ retire
☐ ask for a promotion   ☐ go on for a master's degree   ☐ go on a trip   ☐ get married

Figure it out **B** Complete the sentences using the interviews above to help you.

1. Paul says it _____ be expensive to go to Europe. He's sure about that.

2. Laura thinks she probably _____ get a promotion. She's 95% certain her boss will say no.

3. Christy says she _____ study for a master's degree. She's not sure, though.

4. Laura says she _____ look for a better job. She says it's possible.

5. Joe says he _____ retire next June. He's already decided.

2 Grammar Future with *will, may,* and *might* 🔊 4.23

Extra practice p. 151

You can use *will* to give facts or predictions about the future.

I'**ll** be 65 in June.
It'**ll** be expensive to travel around Europe.
The baby **will** keep us busy!
It **won't** be easy to find a job.

I'll = I will   won't = will not

To show you are not 100% sure about the future, you can use *may* and *might*.

I **may** go on for a master's degree.
I **might not** be able to afford it.

You can also use *will* with expressions like *I guess, I think, maybe,* and *probably*.

We'**ll probably** take some time off from work.
Maybe we'**ll** move to Arizona.

Avoid *will* to talk about plans or decisions already made. Use the present continuous or *be going to*.

I'**m going** to Europe next year. I'**m going to visit** Paris. (NOT ~~I will go to Europe next year. I will visit Paris.~~)

✗ Common errors

Don't use *can* for predictions. Use *may* or *might*.

I **may** go away for vacation.
(NOT I ~~can~~ go away for vacation.)

A Circle the correct options in the conversations below. Compare and practice in groups of three.

1. A What are you going to do at the end of this course?

    B I'm not sure. I guess **I take** / (**I'll take**) another course.

    C I don't know. **I'm going to** / **I may** travel abroad with my brother. He thinks his classes **might** / **can** finish early this year, so we **might** / **will be able to** go in May.

2. A Are your friends going away for vacation next summer?

    B Well, they **'re all going to do** / **will all do** different things. One friend **is going** / **will go** to Istanbul. I'd love to go, too, but I don't know. **I won't** / **I might not** be able to afford it.

    C Four of my friends **will** / **may** be 21, so we **'re having** / **have** a big party. It's going to be fun.

3. A Are you going to look for a new job next year?

    B Actually, I just got a new job. **I'll** / **I'm going to** work for the local newspaper. How about you?

    C I don't know. I think **I'm studying** / **I'll study** for a certificate in nutrition. I mean, **I'll** / **I may** probably go back to school because I'm pretty sure **I won't** / **I might not** get a job.

About you **B** **Group work** Ask and answer the questions. Give your own answers. Who has interesting plans?

3 Speaking naturally Reduction of *will*

Do you think...	*your best friend **will** always be your friend?*	*(friend'll)*
	*the teacher **will** be a millionaire someday?*	*(teacher'll)*
	*your parents **will** ever move to another city?*	*(parents'll)*
	*all your friends **will** have children?*	*(friends'll)*
	*anyone in the class **will** be famous someday?*	*(class'll)*

A 🔊 4.24 Listen and repeat the questions above. Practice the reduction of *will* to *'ll*.

About you **B** **Pair work** Ask and answer the questions. Think of more questions to ask about the future.

A *Do you think your best friend will always be your friend?*
B *Well, we might not always live near each other, but I think we'll always be friends.*

1 Building vocabulary

A **4.25** Listen and say the words. Then make a class list of other jobs and professions. Do you know anyone with these jobs?

"My neighbor is a firefighter. She loves her job."

"My cousin may become a veterinarian at an animal hospital."

> **i Note**
>
> You can also say:
> She works **for** a (computer) company.
> He works **at** a hospital / grocery store.

firefighter · paramedic · police officer · journalist · sales representative · doctor · nurse · dentist · receptionist

computer specialist · letter carrier · business executive · assistant

electrician · carpenter · plumber · architect

Word sort **B** Complete the chart with jobs from above. Add your own ideas. Then compare with a partner.

Who . . .			
has an interesting job?	has a rewarding job?	has a difficult job?	earns a lot of money?
journalists *interior designers*	*nurses*		

"I think journalists have an interesting job. They travel a lot, and . . ."

Vocabulary notebook p. 126

2 Building language

A 🔊 **4.26** Listen. What is Becca's problem? Practice the conversation.

Drew   I can't believe we just have one more year of college!

Becca   I know.

Drew   What are you going to do when you graduate?

Becca   Well, I may go to law school if I get good grades next year.

Drew   Oh, I'm sure you will.

Becca   Well, you never know. My parents will be disappointed if I don't go into law. They're both lawyers.

Drew   Wow. That's a lot of pressure.

Becca   Yeah. And after I graduate, I'll be able to work in their firm.

Drew   Uh-huh. Well, that's good.

Becca   Yeah, but I don't really want to be a lawyer. . . . I want to be a journalist. I guess I need to decide before I go home for the summer.

Drew   Well, good luck!

Figure it out **B** Choose the correct words to complete these sentences about Becca.

1. Becca may go to law school when she **graduates** / **will graduate** from college.

2. If Becca **doesn't** / **won't** go into law, her parents will be disappointed.

3. She needs to decide before she **will go** / **goes** home for the summer.

3 Grammar   Present tense verbs with future meaning 🔊 4.27

Extra practice p. 151

In complex sentences about the future, use the simple present after *if*, *when*, *after*, and *before*.	What are you going to do **when** you **graduate**? **If** I **get** good grades, I may go to law school. My parents will be disappointed **if** I **don't go** into law. **After** I **graduate**, I'll be able to work in their firm. I need to decide **before** I **go** home for the summer.

About you **A** Choose the correct verbs. Then complete the sentences with your own ideas.

1. Before this semester **will be** / **is** over, I think I'll be able to _____ .

2. I'll probably _____ after I **finish** / **will finish** my studies.

3. If I **don't** / **won't** get a good job after I **will graduate** / **graduate**, I might _____ .

4. If I **earn** / **will earn** a lot of money in the next ten years, I may _____ .

5. I'd like to _____ when I **visit** / **will visit** my relatives again.

6. If I **become** / **will become** really fluent in English, I hope I'll be able to _____ .

7. I think I'll _____ after I **retire** / **will retire**.

B Pair work Compare your sentences. Ask your partner questions for more information.

A *Before this semester is over, I think I'll be able to improve my grades.*

B *Good for you. Which subject do you need a better grade in?*

((• **Sounds right** p. 139

1 Conversation strategy Making offers and promises

A Imagine you are planning a barbecue with friends. What things do you put on your "to-do" list?

B 🔊 4.28 Listen. What does Olivia offer to do? How about Jake?

Olivia	I'm really looking forward to the barbecue this weekend.
Jake	Me too. I'll get some steaks, if you like.
Olivia	OK. That sounds good. And I'll bring some salad and stuff. Will you bring some chairs? Oh, and remind me to bring my beach umbrella.
Jake	All right. And I won't forget the drinks this time, either.
Olivia	Good. Uh, do you want me to drive?
Jake	No, I'll drive. You can't afford any more speeding tickets.
Olivia	OK. Then make sure you go to the gas station before you pick me up. We don't want to run out of gas again.
Jake	All right. I will. But hey, we only ran out of gas that one time!

C **Notice** how Olivia and Jake use *I'll* and *I won't* to make offers and promises. Find examples in the conversation.

> *"I'll get some steaks."* (an offer)
> *"I won't forget the drinks."* (a promise)

D Some friends are planning a hiking trip for Saturday. For each comment, find and complete an offer or a promise with *I'll* or *I won't*. Then practice with a partner.

1. How are we going to get there? __b__
2. Do we have to leave early? I might oversleep. _____
3. What food should we take? _____
4. How about something to drink, too? _____
5. Will you remember to bring your GPS? _____
6. Should we check the weather before we go? _____
7. Do we have a trail map? _____

a. Don't worry, _____ call you.
b. I can borrow my parents' car. __I'll__ drive.
c. No, we don't. _____ get one.
d. Just some sandwiches. _____ make them.
e. Probably. _____ look at the forecast.
f. Sure. _____ forget. _____ bring a camera, too.
g. Yeah. _____ buy some bottles of water later.

About you **E** **Pair work** Imagine you are going on a day trip. Choose a place to go. Then take turns asking and answering the questions above. Make offers and promises with *I'll* and *I won't*.

2 Strategy plus *All right* and *OK*

You can use *All right* or *OK* when you agree to something.

Remind me to bring my beach umbrella.

OK.

All right.

In conversation

OK is about six times more frequent than *All right*.

■■■■ *OK.*

■ *All right.*

Respond to the questions with *All right* or *OK*, and make an offer with *I'll*. Then practice with a partner.

1. A Could you help me with my computer? I think it has a virus.

    B _____ . I'll _____ .

2. A I have a favor to ask. Can you give me a ride to class tomorrow?

    B _____ . I'll _____ .

3. A I might get a new tablet this weekend. Can you help me choose one?

    B _____ . I'll _____ .

4. A I'm going to paint my apartment next weekend. Could you help me?

    B _____ . I'll _____ .

    A *Could you help me with my computer? I think it has a virus.*

    B *All right. I'll take a look this afternoon. Is that OK?*

3 Listening and strategies *I'll do it!*

A 🔊 4.29 **Listen to Jack and Helen's conversation. What kind of event are they planning? Where will it take place? When?**

B 🔊 4.29 **Listen again. Complete the sentences. Write *a* to *h*. There is one extra item.**

1. Their mother promises she'll _____ and _____ .

2. Jack says he'll _____ . He says he won't _____ .

3. Helen says she'll _____ . She won't _____ . Helen will also _____ .

a. burn the food	d. send invitations online	g. shop and do the cooking
b. buy a gift and a card	e. get the date wrong	h. pay for everything
c. send a guest list	f. choose the music	

C **Group work** **Plan an end-of-the-year event for your class. Make a list of things to do. Offer and agree to do the different tasks.**

A *We should reserve a room at the school.*

B *OK, I'll call and do that.*

C *And we need to buy some snacks. . . .*

TO DO

Reserve a room at the school.

Buy some snacks.

Lesson D / In the future . . .

1 Reading

A Look at the pictures in the article. Can you guess what inventions the article will describe? Tell the class.

"I think people will use special glasses to get directions."

B Read the article. Which inventions did you already know about? Which were new?

Reading tip

As you read, look for words like *however*, which shows a contrasting idea, and *so*, which sometimes introduces a consequence.

http://www.lifeinthefuture...

WHAT WILL LIFE BE LIKE IN THE FUTURE?

Our analyst says that some weird and wonderful ideas of the future might not be that far away.

1 Smartphones, tablets, and laptops are getting thinner and lighter than ever before. However, in the future, you might not need to carry any gadgets around with you. If designers have their way, you may just need to wear a pair of "virtual goggles" instead. Scientists are testing prototypes at the moment, though it may be some time before they're actually on store shelves.

These goggles will act like a computer screen and display information and entertainment from the Internet.

So, when you are sightseeing, you'll be able to see information about a famous building in front of you. Or you'll be able to get a review of the restaurant menu you're looking at. The goggles will have GPS, so you'll be able to stream directions to a party or locate a nearby coffee shop. They will also have a camera to take photos, and you won't need a cell phone anymore. The goggles will have that built in, too.

2 You might not be able to take a trip into space right now, but in the near future, we may all have access to the outer atmosphere. Private spaceships are taking reservations – at a cost – for flights into space. In the meantime, a Japanese company says it is developing a space

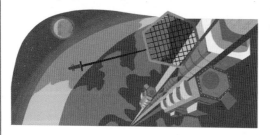

elevator. The elevator, which will carry 30 passengers, will stretch from a base on the ground up to a space station 36,000 kilometers (22,000 miles) above the earth. It will take eight days to reach the space station. Luckily, the elevator will have beds and entertainment on board. The company says it may be ready by 2050.

3 You can already buy mirrors with TVs in them, so you can watch the morning news while you brush your teeth. However, in the future, mirrors will be able to do much, much more. What would you look like with long blond hair? Or with a beard? In the future, you will be able to simply tap your mirror if you want to see yourself with different features. Your mirror will also monitor your health, and it'll be able to tell you when you need a visit to the doctor's office. And before you go to work, you'll be able to set the time for a nice, relaxing bath. Now how hot do you want the water?

C Read the article again. Check (✓) the predictions the article makes.

1. ☐ With "virtual goggles" you'll be able to go online.
2. ☐ These goggles will make it unnecessary for tourists to go sightseeing.
3. ☐ Virtual goggles will have built-in cell phones.
4. ☐ Only trained astronauts will be able to travel on the space elevator.
5. ☐ The space elevator will carry people 22,000 miles above the earth.
6. ☐ The space elevator will probably be ready in the next ten years.
7. ☐ A "smart mirror" will show us what we look like with different hair or features.
8. ☐ With smart mirrors to monitor health, we won't need to go to the doctor.

About you D Pair work If the predictions are correct, will our lives be better or worse? Discuss with a partner.

A *Our lives will be worse with virtual goggles. We'll stop looking at things around us.*

B *I don't really agree. People won't wear the goggles all the time. Just when they need them.*

2 Listening and writing A good idea?

A 🔊 4.30 Listen to Sophia and Alan discuss the inventions from the article on page 124. For each invention, who says it's a good idea? Check (✓) Sophia or Alan.

Invention	Who says it's a good idea?		Why?
	Sophia	**Alan**	
1. virtual goggles	☐	☐	_____
2. a space elevator	☐	☐	_____
3. a smart mirror	☐	☐	_____

About you B 🔊 4.30 Listen again. Write *one* reason why Sophia or Alan thinks the invention is a good idea. Do you agree? Discuss with a partner.

C Read the article below and the Help note. Underline the words that list ideas.

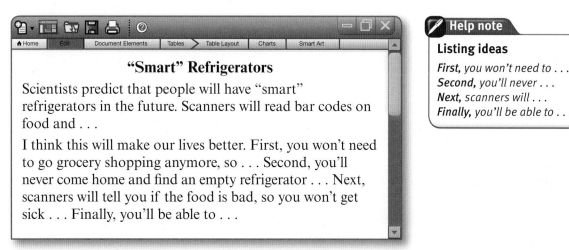

"Smart" Refrigerators

Scientists predict that people will have "smart" refrigerators in the future. Scanners will read bar codes on food and . . .

I think this will make our lives better. First, you won't need to go grocery shopping anymore, so . . . Second, you'll never come home and find an empty refrigerator . . . Next, scanners will tell you if the food is bad, so you won't get sick . . . Finally, you'll be able to . . .

Help note

Listing ideas

First, you won't need to . . .
Second, you'll never . . .
Next, scanners will . . .
Finally, you'll be able to . . .

About you D Write a short article about a future invention. Will it make life better or worse? Why? Give four reasons.

Free talk p. 135

Learning tip *Grouping vocabulary*

Write new vocabulary in groups. You can group words by their endings or by their meanings. You can group expressions by different topic areas.

Talk about jobs

The jobs people mention most in conversation are *lawyer*, *teacher*, and *doctor*.

1 Look at these jobs. Group them by their endings. How many other jobs can you add to each list?

✓ actor	assistant	doctor	journalist	musician	police officer
architect	consultant	electrician	letter carrier	nurse	receptionist
artist	dentist	firefighter	librarian	paramedic	writer

-er / -or	-ant / -ent	-ist	-ian	other
actor				

2 Make a chart like the one below. How many expressions can you write in the chart?

Work	Home and family	Education
get a promotion	have a baby	take an exam

 On your own

Make a list of 20 people you know. What jobs do they do? Write their jobs in English. How many new words do you learn?

Silvio:Clown

Now I can . . .

☑ I can . . .   ? I need to review how to . . .

- ☐ discuss my plans and make predictions.
- ☐ talk about jobs.
- ☐ make offers and promises.
- ☐ agree to offers, requests, and suggestions.

- ☐ understand a conversation about planning events.
- ☐ understand a conversation about inventions.
- ☐ read an article about the future.
- ☐ write an article about a future invention.

1 Who's who?

Austin and Tyler are brothers, but they look very different. Complete the questions for items 1 to 5. Complete items 6 to 9 with comparatives and prepositions. Compare with a partner. Then ask and answer the questions.

1. A _____ alike?
   B No, they look totally different.

2. A _____ like?
   B He's short and heavy, and he's got a mustache.

3. A _____ like – his mother or his father?
   B Austin looks like his mother. She's short, too.

4. A _____ ?
   B He's six feet tall. He's a lot taller than Austin.

5. A _____ ?
   B His eyes are blue.

6. A Do they both have brown hair?
   B Yes, but Tyler's hair is _____ and _____ than Austin's.

7. A Are they both muscular?
   B No, Austin is _____ than Tyler. He works out _____ than Tyler.

8. A Do they both have freckles?
   B Yes, but Tyler has _____ freckles than Austin. Austin probably spends _____ time in the sun.

9. A Is Tyler the one _____ the spiked hair?
   B No, that's Austin. Tyler's the one _____ the ponytail – the one _____ the striped shirt.

Austin   Tyler

2 Can you guess what I mean?

A How many words and expressions can you add to the chart? Compare charts with a partner.

Describing faces	Describing hairstyles	Ways of communicating	Jobs
have freckles	have a ponytail	text someone	electrician

B Pair work Student A: Explain a word or expression to a partner. Student B: Guess the word.

   A *You can do this with your phone or computer.*

   B *Do you mean text someone?*

3 Can you complete this conversation?

Complete the conversation with the words and expressions in the box. Use capital letters where necessary. Practice with a partner. Then role-play the conversation using your own ideas.

all right	I'll	just	wearing	where were we
breaking up	I'll call you back	let's see	what do you call it	with
hold on a second	I've got	✓ this is	what was I saying	you mean

Greg Greg Waters.

Kenji Hello, Greg. _____*This is*_____ Kenji from the office in Tokyo. I was _____ calling to ask . . . What time are you arriving on Monday?

Greg Well, I have my ticket here. _____ , I arrive at, um, 3:30 p.m.

Kenji OK, _____ come to the airport to meet you. Oh, _____ – I've got another call.

Greg _____ . . .

Kenji Hi. Sorry about that. So, _____ ? Oh, yes, I'll meet you. So, how will I recognize you?

Greg Well, I'm tall and _____ blond hair and –

Kenji Sorry, Greg, I can't hear you. You're _____ .

Greg OK. Listen, _____ . . .

Kenji Hi. That's better. So, _____ ?

Greg I was describing myself. So, um, I'll be the blond guy _____ the sunglasses, _____ a USA T-shirt.

Kenji Um, OK. Maybe I should wear a – _____ ? A thing with my name on it so you can find me?

Greg Oh, _____ a badge. Good idea!

4 Future plans and dreams

A Circle the correct options, and then complete the sentences with true information.

1. When **I'll get / I get** home tonight, I'm going to _____ , and I might _____ , but I probably won't _____ .

2. If **you'll want / you want** help with your homework this weekend, **I'll help / I help** you. I'm not _____ on Saturday, but I may _____ on Sunday.

3. If **I'll win / I win** the lottery this year, I promise **I'll buy / I buy** all my classmates dinner. I'll also _____ , and I might _____ , too.

4. If I ever **will become / become** famous, I **won't / don't** change. **I'll still be / I'm still** myself, and I won't _____ .

B Pair work Tell each other your sentences. Can you continue the conversations?

UNIT 7 Travel smart!

1 Look at the pictures. What advice do you have for Traveler B in each situation? Make a list.

2 **Role play** Now imagine you and your partner are in the situations above. Take turns giving and responding to advice.

A *You know, maybe you shouldn't leave your money in your pocket like that.*

B *Oh, yeah, I guess. But I don't have a wallet.*

A *Why don't you go to that shop to look for a new wallet?*

UNIT **8** **All about home**

1 **Pair work** Discuss the questions. Find three ways you're alike. Find three ways you're different.

1. What's your room like at home?
   - What do you have on your walls?
   - Do you have a TV in your room?
   - Would you like to change your room? What would you change?
2. Are you neat or messy at home?
   - Do you make your bed every morning?
   - Do you leave things on top of dressers, tables, and chairs? Or do you put everything in drawers or a closet?
   - Is there a lot of clutter in your house? Whose clutter is it?

3. Do you prefer a quiet or a noisy home?
   - When you listen to music, do you use headphones or speakers?
   - Do you sing along with the music?
   - Do you leave the TV on when you're not watching?
4. Do you or your family do a "spring cleaning" every year?
   - Who does most of the work?
   - What do you do?
5. Do you have any unusual habits at home?

2 **Group work** Join another pair. Tell them about yourself and your partner.

"Mario and I both have small rooms, but he has posters of his favorite rock band on the wall. I just have some pictures of my friends and family on my desk."

Free talk

What was happening?

Pair work Look at the picture. Bob just crashed into a lamppost. Some other people saw the accident. What were they doing when it happened? What was Bob doing? Study the picture and try to remember as many details as possible. Then turn to Free talk 9B on page 136.

UNIT
10 **Which is better?**

Pair work What are the advantages and disadvantages of the choices below? Which is better? Give at least three reasons for each choice. Discuss with your partner.

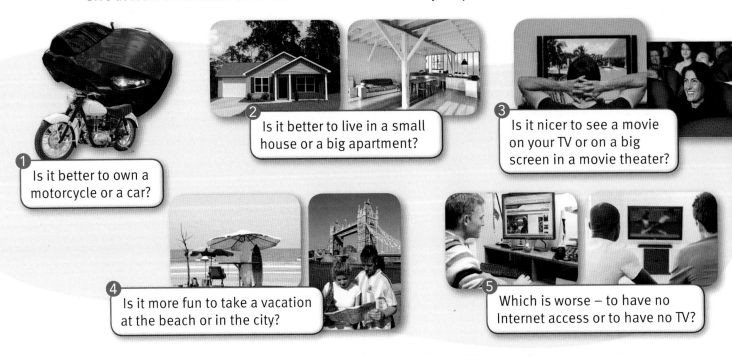

1 Is it better to own a motorcycle or a car?

2 Is it better to live in a small house or a big apartment?

3 Is it nicer to see a movie on your TV or on a big screen in a movie theater?

4 Is it more fun to take a vacation at the beach or in the city?

5 Which is worse – to have no Internet access or to have no TV?

A *Well, I think it's better to own a motorcycle than a car – and it's more fun.*

B *Actually, I agree. It's also easier to find parking spaces when you have a motorcycle.*

A *And it's just cheaper. Cars use more gas.*

UNIT 11A What's different?

Pair work Student A: These people are at the mall on Saturday morning. Your partner has a picture of the same people on Saturday afternoon. In that picture, each person is different in two ways. Ask questions to find out what's different. Where did each person go?

A *Do you see the woman with the dark hair?*

B *Yes. Is she wearing a blue dress in your picture?*

A *Yes, she is. So that's the same. Does she have a ponytail in your picture?*

B *No, she doesn't. Her hair is short. So that's different.*

A *I guess she went to the hair salon.*

UNIT 12 I might do that.

Pair work Write your answers to the questions in the chart. Then compare answers with a partner. Ask questions to find out more information and continue the conversations.

Can you think of . . .	My answers
1. something you may do when you get home tonight?	
2. someone you'll probably see next week?	
3. something you might do next year?	
4. something new you'd like to try?	
5. a place you might visit in the next five years?	
6. something you think you'll do if you earn a lot of money?	
7. something you might do when you retire?	
8. something you'll probably never do in your life?	

A *OK. So, I may cook myself a nice dinner tonight if I'm not too tired.*

B *Nice. What do you think you'll cook?*

A *Oh, maybe some pasta or something.*

B *I have a great recipe for pasta. I'll find it for you.*

A *All right. Thanks.*

Free talk

What was happening?

1 Pair work How much do you remember about the picture in Free talk 9A on page 134? Discuss the questions with a partner. Do you agree on the answers?

1. What was Bob doing when he crashed? What did he crash into?
2. What else was he doing?
3. What color were his sneakers?
4. What else was he wearing?
5. Was he wearing a helmet?
6. How many people saw the accident?
7. What was the young boy holding in his hand?
8. What happened when the boy saw the accident?
9. What was the man at the flower shop doing?
10. What was the man wearing? What did he shout?
11. What were the girls in the café doing when Bob hit the lamppost?
12. What were the girls wearing?
13. What was the woman in front of the grocery store carrying?
14. What did she do when Bob passed her?
15. How many other details can you remember?

A *I think he was riding a scooter.*

B *Actually, I'm pretty sure he was riding a skateboard. OK. What did he crash into?*

2 Pair work Now look at the picture in Free talk 9A again to check your answers. How many did you get right?

What's different?

Pair work Student B: These people are at the mall on Saturday afternoon. Your partner has a picture of the same people on Saturday morning. In that picture, each person is different in two ways. Ask questions to find out what's different. Where did each person go?

A *Do you see the woman with the dark hair?*

B *Yes. Is she wearing a blue dress in your picture?*

A *Yes, she is. So that's the same. Does she have a ponytail in your picture?*

B *No, she doesn't. Her hair is short. So that's different.*

A *I guess she went to the hair salon.*

Sounds right

UNIT 7 🔊 **4.37** Listen and repeat the words. Check (✓) the words that have a silent letter *l*.

1. ☑ cou_ld   3. ☐ mi_lk   5. ☐ sa_lmon   7. ☐ si_lk   9. ☐ wa_lk
2. ☐ he_lp   4. ☐ o_ld   6. ☐ shou_ld   8. ☐ ta_lk   10. ☐ wou_ld

UNIT 8 🔊 **4.38** Listen and repeat the words. Notice the underlined sounds. Match the words with the same underlined sounds.

1. j<u>e</u>welry __e__

2. ni<u>gh</u>tstand _____

3. <u>o</u>ven _____

4. sh<u>ow</u>er _____

5. s<u>o</u>fa _____

a. m<u>i</u>crowave

b. r<u>ou</u>nd

c. st<u>o</u>ve

d. st<u>u</u>ff

e. s<u>ui</u>t

UNIT 9 🔊 **4.39 Listen and repeat the sentences. Notice the underlined sounds. Check (✓) the verbs that have an extra syllable and end in /ɪd/.**

1. ☐ I call<u>ed</u> for help.
2. ☐ I sprain<u>ed</u> my wrist.
3. ☐ I delet<u>ed</u> my photos.
4. ☐ I damag<u>ed</u> the car.
5. ☐ It happen<u>ed</u> last week.
6. ☐ I wait<u>ed</u> an hour.

UNIT 10 🔊 **4.40 Listen and repeat the words. Notice the underlined sounds. Are the sounds like the sound in _see_ or _zero_? Write _s_ or _z_.**

1. alway<u>s</u> _z_
2. bu<u>s</u>y ____
3. busine<u>ss</u> ____
4. call<u>s</u> ____
5. con<u>c</u>ert ____
6. ea<u>s</u>ier ____
7. expen<u>s</u>ive ____
8. le<u>ss</u> ____
9. me<u>ss</u>age ____
10. ni<u>c</u>er ____
11. <u>s</u>pam ____
12. wor<u>s</u>e ____

UNIT 11 🔊 **4.41 Listen and repeat the words. Notice the underlined sounds. Match the words with the same underlined sounds.**

1. c<u>or</u>nrows ____
2. fr<u>e</u>ckles ____
3. m<u>u</u>stache ____
4. sh<u>a</u>ved ____
5. p<u>ie</u>rced ____
6. w<u>ea</u>r ____
7. bl<u>ou</u>se ____

a. b<u>ea</u>rd
b. br<u>ai</u>ds
c. h<u>ai</u>r
d. br<u>ow</u>n
e. h<u>ea</u>d
f. m<u>u</u>scular
g. sh<u>or</u>t

UNIT 12 🔊 **4.42 Listen and repeat the words. Notice that some syllables are weak like the /ə/ sound in _away_ or the /ər/ sound in _dinner_. Other syllables are strong, like the syllable _sis_ in _assistant_. Circle the stressed (strongest) syllable.**

1. as(sis)tant
2. carrier
3. doctor
4. journalist
5. letter
6. officer
7. paramedic
8. promotion
9. police
10. representative

Extra practice

UNIT
7 **Lesson A** Infinitives for reasons; *It's* + adjective + *to* . . .

A Correct the conversations. Pay attention to infinitives for reasons and *It's / Is it* + adjective + *to*.

1. A Do you ever go online ^to^ buy train or bus tickets?
   B Well, I buy train tickets online because expensive buy them at the train station.

2. A Do you use a credit card or a debit card pay for things online?
   B A debit card. I'm only 17, and is just not possible get a credit card at my age.

3. A Do you have to travel far visit your family?
   B Well, my grandparents live about three hours away. So we take the bus go and see them. It's a long trip, but that's OK. I think is important see your family.

4. A Do you think it's fun travel alone?
   B It depends. I guess it nice have a friend with you when you go sightseeing.

5. A Is easy to get around in your town?
   B It's pretty easy. You can take the subway get to most places. It's fast and cheap.

6. A What do you do on the weekends relax?
   B I like to go to the beach go windsurfing.

About you **B** Write your own answers to the questions. Then ask and answer the questions with a partner.

UNIT
7 **Lesson B** Advice and suggestions

> **✕ Common errors**
>
> Do not leave out *to* after *need*.
>
> You **need to take** a toothbrush. (NOT You ~~need take a . . .~~)

A Circle the correct words to complete the conversations. Then compare with a partner. Do you agree with the advice?

1. A I have to fly on Friday, but I have a cold. What **I should / should I** do?
   B Well, you probably shouldn't **go / to go** to work. Just **stay / staying** home and don't **go / to go** out. And don't forget **take / to take** some cold medicine on the plane with you.

2. A I'm going camping next weekend. Should I **take / to take** insect repellent?
   B Oh, you definitely need **have / to have** some this time of year. It's probably **good idea / a good idea** to take some shirts with long sleeves, too. And why **don't you / you don't** take something for bites in your first-aid kit?

3. A We're going to the beach next weekend. What **need / should** I take with me?
   B Well, you should **take / taking** an umbrella. It gets hot. And you probably need **pack / to pack** a picnic. The cafés are expensive. And **do you want / do you want to** take a volleyball? It's fun to play volleyball on the beach.

About you **B** **Pair work** Write two of your own suggestions for each question above. Take turns asking the questions and making suggestions.

UNIT **8** **Lesson A** *Whose . . . ?*; Possessive pronouns

Complete the questions with *whose* and a verb. Then complete the conversation with possessive pronouns. Practice with a partner.

1. Teacher   I can hear a cell phone! Uh, __*whose*__ phone __*is*__ it?
   Student   Oh, I'm really sorry. It's __*mine*__ . . . . Sorry. I just turned it off.

2. Teacher   I think someone left a backpack. _____ backpack _____ under that chair?
   Student   Um, Mario has a backpack like that. I think it's _____ .

3. Teacher   Two people forgot to write their names on the test. _____ tests _____ these?
   Student   Let's see. That looks like Angela's handwriting. It's probably _____ . Oh, and
             that's _____ . Sorry I forgot to put my name on it.

4. Teacher   I found these glasses last week after class. _____ glasses _____ they?
   Student   Well, Manuel usually wears glasses in class. Maybe they're _____ .
   Teacher   Excuse me, Manuel. I think these are _____ .

5. Teacher   _____ science project _____ this? Does anyone know?
   Student   Oh, it's Dana and Pam's. Well, I *think* it's _____ .

UNIT **8** **Lesson B** Order of adjectives; pronouns *one* and *ones*

> **✕ Common errors**
>
> Use *one* for a singular noun and *ones* for a plural noun.
>
> *I want to buy a new cell phone. Which **one** should I get?*
> (NOT *Which ~~ones~~ should I get?*)

Complete these conversations with the pronouns *one* or *ones*.
Unscramble the last sentences. Then practice with a partner.

1. A   I need to buy a new water bottle. Should I buy a plastic _____ or a metal _____ ?
   B   You can get some really cool _____ . get / You / metal / nice / should / a / one
       _____ .

2. A   I think shoes are expensive. Maybe because I always buy expensive leather _____ .
   B   I know a great discount store. shoes / leather / buy / inexpensive / You / can / there
       _____ .

3. A   You needed a new tablet cover, right? Did you find a nice _____ ?
   B   Uh-huh. red / one / found / plastic / I / a / pretty
       _____ .

4. A   I need new pants for the winter. Which _____ should I buy? Some wool pants or those cotton
       _____ ?
   B   Well, wool is nice. get / You / some / pants / should / wool / black
       _____ .

5. A   What kind of rug did you buy for your bedroom? A Turkish _____ ?
   B   Actually, I decided to buy something different. beautiful / I / a / Indian / rug / bought / little
       _____ .

Lesson A Past continuous statements

A Complete the sentences with the past continuous or the simple past. Compare with a partner.

1. I was in class last week, and the teacher _was explaining_ (explain) something, and I just
   ___fell___ (fall) asleep. When I _____ (wake up), I realized that everyone _____ (look)
   at me.

2. Yesterday I _____ (walk) down the street, and I _____ (text) a friend when
   I _____ (walk) right into a lamppost. I guess I _____ (not pay) attention.

3. My sister and her husband _____ (carry) some dishes into the kitchen when they both
   _____ (trip) over a rug. They _____ (drop) and _____ (break) all their new dishes!

4. Last week a friend of mine _____ (invite) me over for dinner. In the afternoon, when
   she _____ (cook), she _____ (pick up) a heavy pot and _____ (hurt) her back.
   When I _____ (arrive), she _____ (lie) on the sofa, so I _____ (make) dinner for us!

5. The other day, a friend and I were at my house. We _____ (not / do) anything special, so
   I _____ (say), "Come on. Let's go out for coffee. It's on me." While I _____ (wait) in line to
   order, I _____ (realize) I didn't have my wallet. So my friend _____ (pay) for everything.
   I was really embarrassed.

About you B Choose two of the situations above and rewrite them with your own information.

I was in class last week, and my friend was sending a text when the teacher asked him a question.

Lesson B Past continuous questions; reflexive pronouns

> **✕ Common errors**
>
> Use the past continuous,
> not the simple past, for
> longer actions.
>
> *When I **was making** dinner,
> a friend called.*
> (NOT *When I ~~made~~ dinner,
> a friend called.*)

A Complete the questions in the conversations and add reflexive pronouns. Practice with a partner.

1. A I accidentally burned ___myself___ when I was cooking dinner.
   B Oh, no! What _were you making_ (make)?
   A I was making a vegetable curry.

2. A My sister hurt _____ at the gym last night. She sprained her ankle.
   B That's too bad. _____ (do) aerobics?
   A No, she was doing yoga. I guess you can hurt _____ if you're not careful.

3. A Was there anyone fun at the party last night? I mean, who _____ (talk) to?
   B Oh, this really boring guy. He talked about _____ the whole time. I didn't talk
      about _____ once!

4. A When I got home last night, my kids were arguing.
   B Really? What _____ (fight) about?
   A Who should do the dishes. I just can't leave them by _____ .

5. A There was a lot of noise when I called you last night. What _____ (do)?
   B Last night? I was having dinner with some friends at a restaurant. We were really
      enjoying _____ .

About you B Pair work Think of situations like the ones above. Tell a partner what happened.

"I accidentally burned myself when I was camping last summer."

UNIT
10 **Lesson A** Comparative adjectives

A Complete these questions with the comparative forms of the adjectives (↑ = more; ↓ = less). Compare with a partner. Then write an answer for each question.

In your opinion . . .

1. Which is _____less expensive_____ (expensive ↓), an e-reader or a tablet?
   An e-reader is less expensive than a tablet, but a tablet is more useful.

2. Is it _____ (easy ↑) to read an e-book or a regular book outside?
   _____

3. Which is _____ (useful ↑), a cell phone or a tablet?
   _____

4. Is it _____ (difficult ↓) to write an email on a laptop or on a smartphone?
   _____

5. Which is _____ (nice ↑) for personal messages, email or a social network?
   _____

6. Is it _____ (bad ↑) to lose your laptop or your phone?
   _____

7. Is it _____ (good ↑) to hold your cell phone or use an earpiece when you call someone?
   _____

8. Why are phone calls becoming _____ (popular ↓) than text messages?
   _____

About you **B** **Pair work** Take turns asking and answering the questions. Give reasons for your opinions.

UNIT
10 **Lesson B** *More, less, fewer*

> ✖ **Common errors**
>
> Use *than* after a comparative, not *that* or *then*.
>
> *Texting is quicker **than** calling.* (NOT *Texting is quicker ~~that~~ calling.*)

A Complete the sentences with *more*, *less*, or *fewer*. Then compare with a partner.

1. I'm spending _____less_____ time on my social network these days because I'm very busy at work.

2. I'm getting _____ exercise now because I'm walking home from work every day.

3. My friends and I text each other very late at night, so I'm sleeping _____ than I should.

4. My friends prefer texting to email, so they're sending me _____ email messages these days.

5. I don't have much time to cook, so I'm eating out _____ than I did before.

6. I don't like big groups. I enjoy myself _____ when I have dinner with just one or two close friends.

7. I feel a bit shy in groups. I usually talk _____ than other people.

8. In my family, we're watching TV _____ together because we're all spending more and more time on our laptops.

9. I'm buying _____ newspapers now because I'm getting my news online.

About you **B** **Pair work** Are the sentences above true for you? Discuss with your partner.

"I think I'm spending more time on my social network these days. I have more and more friends – around 500 now."

Extra practice

UNIT 11 Lesson A Describing people; *have got*

About you Write questions for the answers. Practice with a partner. Then ask and answer the questions, giving your own information.

> **✗ Common errors**
>
> Do not use *look like* before an adjective.
>
> He **looks** tired.
> (NOT He ~~looks like~~ tired.)

1. A _____ , your mother or your father?
    B I think I look more like my mother.

2. A _____ ?
    B My father's hair is dark brown.

3. A _____ ?
    B No, she doesn't. She's got very straight hair.

4. A _____ ?
    B My mother? She's about one meter seventy-five (five foot seven).

5. A _____ ?
    B My best friend? He's tall and thin, and he's got curly black hair.

6. A _____ ?
    B No, we don't look alike. My friend is a lot taller than I am.

UNIT 11 Lesson B Phrases with the verb + *-ing* and prepositions

A Someone is asking questions about the people in the photo. Unscramble the sentences. Label the people. Then practice with a partner.

1. A the / with / the / blond hair / tall / who's / guy
    _____ ?
    B That's Adrian. He's about six foot four.

2. A woman / who's / standing / the / him / next to
    _____ ?
    B Angela. She's in my math class.

3. A wearing / the / woman / yellow / the / top / blond / who's
    _____ ?
    B That's Abby. She's a good friend of Daniel's.

4. A Daniel? Is he in the picture?
    B Yeah. the / he's / shaved head / guy / with / the
    _____ ?

5. A Is your friend Gina in the picture? Which one is she?
    B top / the / in / she's / orange / woman / the
    _____ ?

B Pair work Ask and answer questions about the people in the photo.

"Which one is Adrian?"   *"Who's the woman wearing the orange top?"*

150

UNIT
12 Lesson A Future with *will*, *may*, and *might*

A Read the questions about future plans and choose the best options in the answers. Then practice with a partner.

1. A Are you going to the beach on Saturday?
    B Probably not. It looks like **it'll rain / it rains** all weekend.

2. A Do you have plans to move to a new apartment?
    B Actually, **I'll move / I'm moving** next week – I just found a new place!

3. A Are you going to take another English course next semester?
    B I'm not sure. **I might not / I won't** have enough time.

4. A How are you going to celebrate your next birthday?
    B Well, **I'll be / I may be** 30 on my next birthday, but I don't think **I'll / I may** do anything special.

5. A Do you think you'll travel abroad in the next couple of years?
    B I don't know. Maybe **I'll go / I go** to Spain to learn Spanish.

6. A Do you think you'll be rich someday?
    B No. I know **I won't / I may not** be rich because I'm not very good with money.

About you **B Pair work Ask and answer the questions. Give your own information.**

UNIT
12 Lesson B Present tense verbs with future meaning

A Choose the best expressions to complete these questions. Then compare with a partner.

1. Are you going to do anything interesting after class **will be / is** over today?
2. After you **will eat / eat** dinner tonight, are you going to do any work?
3. What do you think **you'll do / you do** before you go to bed tonight?
4. If you **don't / won't** fall asleep right away, do you think you'll read for a while?
5. What's the first thing you're going to do when **you'll get up / you get up** tomorrow morning?
6. Are you going to exercise tomorrow before **you'll have / you have** breakfast?
7. If it **doesn't / won't** rain tomorrow, do you think you'll go running or go for a walk?
8. Are you going to meet your friends tomorrow when you **get out / will get out** of class?
9. If you **don't / won't** have time to eat breakfast at home tomorrow, will you have an early lunch?
10. If you **will go out / go out** this weekend, where will you go?

About you **B Pair work Ask and answer the questions. What do you have in common?**

Illustration credits

Harry Briggs: 27, 79, 95, 100, 101, 134 **Bunky Hurter:** 10, 20, 30, 42, 52, 62 *(bottom)*, 74, 84, 94, 106, 116, 126 **Cambridge University Press:** 47 *(bottom left border)*, 55, 66 *(top right)*, 94 *(top)* **Kim Johnson:** 25, 81, 91, 128, 132 **Scott Macneil:** 18, 54, 56, 60, 62 *(top)*, 145 **Frank Montagna:** 28, 124, 135, 136 **Q2A studio artists:** 69, 86, 111, 120 **Gavin Reece:** 31, 87, 103, 121 **Lucy Truman:** 4, 89, 96, 108, 127

Photography credits

Back cover: ©vovan/Shutterstock **16, 17, 58, 59, 80, 90, 91, 102, 103, 122, 123** ©Cambridge University Press **6, 7, 26, 27, 34, 38, 39, 44, 48, 49, 70, 71, 76, 112, 113** ©Frank Veronsky **viii** *(left)* ©Rich Legg/Getty Images/RF; *(right)* ©Image Source/SuperStock **1** *(clockwise from top left)* ©Corbis/SuperStock; ©Asia Images/SuperStock; ©Jesse Wild/Total Guitar magazine/Getty Images; ©Thinkstock **2** AsiaPix/SuperStock **3** ©Thinkstock **5** *(left to right)* ©Blue Jean Images/SuperStock; *(tv)* ©Pakhnyushcha/Shutterstock; *(news)* ©Heather Wines/CBS via Getty Images; ©Flirt/SuperStock; ©GoodMood Photo/istockphoto **7** *(bottom)* ©kristian sekulic/istockphoto **8** *(left)* ©Steve Debenport/istockphoto; *(right)* ©Thinkstock **9** ©Chris Pecoraro/istockphoto **11** *(top row, left to right)* ©photovideostock/istockphoto; ©Nadya Lukic/istockphoto; ©YinYang/istockphoto *(bottom row, left to right)* ©Alberto Pomares/istockphoto; ©Ken Babione/istockphoto; ©Thinkstock; *(tablet)* ©L_amica/Shutterstock **12** ©Don Bayley/Getty Images/RF; *(background)* ©Feng Yu/Shutterstock **14** *(top row, left to right)* ©Kevin Mazur/WireImage/Getty Images; ©Kevin Mazur/WireImage/Getty Images; ©George Pimentel/WireImage/Getty Images; ©Lucas Jackson/Reuters/Corbis *(bottom row, left to right)* ©Handout/WireImage/Getty Images; ©Roberta Parkin/Redferns via Getty Images; ©David Redfern/Redferns/Getty Images; ©TIZIANA FABI/AFP/Getty Images **15** ©Dougal Waters Photography Ltd/Getty Images/RF **17** *(bottom, left to right)* ©Casey McNamara/Getty Images; ©Charlie Neuman/ZUMA Press/Corbis; ©Exactostock/SuperStock; ©Thomas Trötscher/istockphoto **18** *(top to bottom)* ©Tyler Olson/Shutterstock; ©nimu1956/istockphoto **19** ©Ridofranz/istockphoto **21** *(clockwise from top left)* ©Alex Brosa/Getty Images; ©Design Pics/SuperStock; ©Chris Schmidt/Getty Images; ©Belinda Images/SuperStock; ©Nicolas McComber/istockphoto; ©Cultura Limited/SuperStock **22** *(top row, left to right)* ©Jamie Carroll/istockphoto; ©Fotolia; ©Thinkstock *(bottom row, left to right)* ©digitalskillet/istockphoto; ©Thinkstock; ©Asia Images/SuperStock; *(background)* ©Natutik/Shutterstock **23** ©Elena Ray/Shutterstock **24** *(top row, left to right)* ©age fotostock/SuperStock; ©B BOISSONNET/BSIP/SuperStock; ©MAY/BSIP/SuperStock; ©laflor/istockphoto *(bottom row, left to right)* ©Blend Images/SuperStock; ©Jens Koenig/Getty Images; ©flyfloor/Getty Images; ©Science Photo Library/SuperStock **25** ©DEX IMAGE/Getty Images/RF **29** *(top row, left to right)* ©Thinkstock; ©Thinkstock; ©age fotostock/SuperStock; ©Alexander Fortelny/istockphoto; *(middle, all photos)* ©Thinkstock; *(bottom, left to right)* ©Thinkstock; ©Silvia Jansen/istockphoto **33** *(clockwise from top left)* ©Thinkstock; ©Image Source/Getty Images; ©SuperStock; ©Cultura Limited/SuperStock; ©Andres Rodriguez/SuperFusion/SuperStock; ©Cusp/SuperStock **35** ©age fotostock/SuperStock **36** *(top row, left to right)* ©Thinkstock; ©Donna Coleman/istockphoto; ©Blue Jean Images/SuperStock *(bottom row, left to right)* ©bikeriderlondon/Shutterstock; ©Exactostock/SuperStock; ©Burke/Triolo Productions/Getty Images **37** ©hanibaram/istockphoto **39** *(bottom, left to right)* ©Charlie Neuman/ZUMA Press/Corbis; ©Christophe Boisvieux/Corbis **40** *(left to right)* ©AP Photo/Larry Crowe; ©Benjamin Loo/istockphoto; ©Jupiterimages/Getty Images/RF; *(background)* ©Paprika/Shutterstock **41** *(background)* ©Devor/Shutterstock **42** *(notebook background)* ©Elena Schweitzer/Shutterstock **43** *(clockwise from top left)* ©age fotostock/SuperStock; ©LEMOINE/BSIP/SuperStock; ©Blend Images/SuperStock; ©Fancy Collection/SuperStock **46** *(top row, left to right)* ©Nancy Louie/istockphoto; ©Fancy Collection/SuperStock; *(bottom row, left to right)* ©Juanmonino/istockphoto; ©Fancy Collection/SuperStock **47** *(top row, left to right)* ©Picsfive/Shutterstock; © dafne/Shutterstock; ©Thinkstock *(bottom row, left to right)* ©hh5800/istockphoto; ©Christopher Futcher/istockphoto; ©Thinkstock **49** *(bottom)* ©Cusp/SuperStock **50** ©Ron Levine/Getty Images **51** ©Thinkstock **53** *(clockwise from top right)* ©Jupiterimages/Thinkstock; ©Exactostock/SuperStock; ©age fotostock/SuperStock; ©Henry Westheim Photography/Alamy **57** ©Thinkstock **59** *(bottom)* ©Ivan Solis/istockphoto **60** *(top to bottom)* ©Thinkstock; ©Reimar Gaertner/age fotostock/SuperStock; *(background)* ©Thinkstock **61** *(top to bottom)* ©GUIZIOU Franck/hemi/Hemis.fr/SuperStock; ©freesoulproduction/Shutterstock **63** ©imagebroker.net/SuperStock **65** *(clockwise from top left)* ©Glow Images - 40260.com/SuperStock; ©Thomas Sztanek/Purestock/SuperStock; ©Fancy Collection/SuperStock; ©Maskot/Getty Images **66** ©Wendy Carter/istockphoto **67** ©Beyond/SuperStock **68** *(bathing suit)* ©sagir/Shutterstock; *(sandals)* ©Shevel Artur/Shutterstock; *(towel)* ©Mike Flippo/Shutterstock; *(cooler)* ©Danny E Hooks/Shutterstock; *(hat)* ©windu/Shutterstock; *(mp3 player)* ©Thinkstock; *(sunglasses)* ©Uros Zunic/Shutterstock; *(insect repellent)* ©andrea crisante/Shutterstock; *(tent)* ©trekandshoot/Shutterstock; *(GPS)* ©Thinkstock; *(camera)* ©Chiyacat/Shutterstock; *(scissors)* ©Phakkaphon Juawanich/Shutterstock; *(sleeping bag)* ©Mark Herreid/Shutterstock; *(first-aid kit)* ©Alan Crawford/istockphoto; *(pajamas)* ©Suljo/istockphoto; *(tablet computer)* ©Sashkin/Shutterstock; *(flashlight)* ©Artur Marfin/istockphoto; *(batteries)* ©grekoff/Shutterstock; *(charger)* ©zirconicusso/Shutterstock; *(e-reader)* ©Ziva_K/istockphoto; *(brush)* ©FomaA/Shutterstock; *(hair dryer)* ©Nordling/Shutterstock; *(makeup)* ©Sergiy Kuzmin/Shutterstock; *(shampoo)* ©Alex011973/Shutterstock; *(soap)* ©Robert Red/Shutterstock; *(razor)* ©Lusoimages/Shutterstock; *(toothpaste)* ©Kenneth C. Zirkel/istockphoto; *(toothbrush)* ©George Dolgikh/Shutterstock; *(sunscreen)* ©Africa Studio/Shutterstock **71** *(bottom)* ©Exactostock/SuperStock **72** *(top to bottom)* ©Fotostudio Jaap Woets; ©EcoCamp Patagonia; ©The Safari Collection; *(tablet)* ©L_amica/Shutterstock **73** *(top row, left to right)* ©Hugh Rooney/Eye Ubiquitous/Corbis; ©Derek Croucher/Getty Images; ©imagebroker.net/SuperStock *(bottom)* ©Fotolia; *(background)* ©Nik Merkulov/Shutterstock **75** *(clockwise from top right)* ©Lisa F. Young/istockphoto; ©Digital Vision/Thinkstock; ©Lucas Allen/Corbis; ©Sheltered Images/SuperStock **77** ©peepo/istockphoto **78** *(clockwise from top left)* ©Thinkstock; ©Thinkstock; ©Frank Short/Istockphoto; ©Elena Elisseeva/Shutterstock **82** ©Don Farrall/Getty Images **83** *(top row, left to right)* ©Hans Laubel/istockphoto; *(news)* ©John Paul Filo/CBS vis Getty Images; ©George Doyle/Thinkstock; ©Tatyana Nyshko/istockphoto; ©RelaXimages/SuperStock; *(bottom row, left to right)* ©moodboard/SuperStock; ©Stephen Chiang/Getty Images; ©Image Source/SuperStock; ©Artazum/Shutterstock **84** *(left to right)* ©Ramsey Blacklock/istockphoto; ©ShutterWorx/istockphoto; ©Sawayasu Tsuji/istockphoto; ©Yenwen Lu/istockphoto **85** *(clockwise from top right)* ©Paula Connelly/istockphoto; ©Exactostock/SuperStock; ©Exactostock/SuperStock; ©Tom England/istockphoto **86** *(top to bottom)* ©Thinkstock; ©Thinkstock; ©Maria Teijeiro/Thinkstock **88** *(main photo)* ©Exactostock/SuperStock; *(top to bottom)* ©Kasiap/Shutterstock; ©Thinkstock; ©Thinkstock; ©Levent Konuk/Shutterstock; ©wavebreakmedia/Shutterstock **92** *(clockwise from top left)* ©Thinkstock; ©Thinkstock; ©Jupiterimages/Thinkstock; ©Stockbyte/Thinkstock **97** *(clockwise from top left)* ©Hocus Focus Studio/istockphoto; ©Exactostock/SuperStock; ©Exactostock/SuperStock; ©Radius/SuperStock; ©Blend Images/SuperStock; ©Exactostock/SuperStock; *(inset)* Shelly Perry/istockphoto **98** *(top row, left to right)* ©Jon Feingersh/MediaBakery; ©SZE FEI WONG/istockphoto; ©laflor/istockphoto; *(bottom row, left to right)* ©George Doyle/Thinkstock; *(inset)* ©Exactostock/SuperStock; ©BananaStock/Thinkstock **104** *(tablet)* ©L_amica/Shutterstock **107** ©Steve Debenport/istockphoto **110** *(top row, left to right)* ©Goldmund Lukic/istockphoto; ©Michael Bodmann/istockphoto; ©laflor/istockphoto; ©Fancy Collection/SuperStock; *(middle row, left to right)* ©Junko Yokoyama/Getty Images; ©Sanjay Deva/istockphoto; ©James Woodson/Thinkstock; ©Amos Morgan/Thinkstock; *(bottom row, left to right)* ©Jamie Choy/istockphoto; ©wrangel/istockphoto; ©Exactostock/SuperStock; ©Fancy Collection/SuperStock **112** *(bottom)* ©Jim Barber/Shutterstock **113** *(bottom, left to right)* ©vipflash/Shutterstock; ©Leonard Adam/Getty Images; ©Venturelli/Getty Images for P&G Prestige; ©Henry S. Dziekan III/Getty Images; ©s_bukley/Shutterstock; ©Francois Durand/Getty Images **114** *(top to bottom)* ©Thinkstock; ©selimaksan/istockphoto; ©Todd Smith istockphoto; ©AlexKol Photography/Shutterstock; ©coloroftime/istockphoto; ©sam100/Shutterstock; ©Radu Razvan/istockphoto **117** *(clockwise from top right)* ©Westend61/SuperStock; ©Westend61/SuperStock; ©Fancy Collection/SuperStock; ©Ocean/Corbis **118** *(clockwise from top right)* ©Christopher Futcher/istockphoto; ©Thinkstock; ©Juergen Bosse/istockphoto; ©Thinkstock; ©YinYang/istockphoto **123** *(bottom)* ©Yong Hian Lim/istockphoto **124** *(background)* ©URRRA/Shutterstock **129** *(left to right)* ©Belinda Images/SuperStock; ©Thinkstock; ©YinYang/istockphoto **130** ©Elena Kalistratova/istockphoto **131** ©Aleksandrs Gorins/istockphoto **133** ©Oleg Zabielin/Shutterstock **134** *(top row, left to right)* ©ewg3D/istockphoto; ©Henrik Jonsson/istockphoto; ©Linda Johnsonbaugh/istockphoto; ©zveiger alexandre/istockphoto; ©DrGrounds/istockphoto; ©Rich Legg/istockphoto; *(bottom row, left to right)* ©Yulia Popkova/istockphoto; ©Jon Arnold/Jon Arnold Images/SuperStock; ©LEMOINE/BSIP/SuperStock; ©Stockbroker/SuperStock **150** ©michaeljung/Shutterstock

Text credits

While every effort has been made, it has not always been possible to identify the sources of all the materials used, or to trace the copyright holders. If any omissions are brought to our notice, we will be happy to include the appropriate acknowledgements on reprinting.

50 Interview used with permission of Joseph Hodgson.